You Can't Teach That!

The Battle over University Classrooms

KEITH E. WHITTINGTON

polity

First published in 2024 by Polity Press

Polity Press
65 Bridge Street
Cambridge CB2 1UR, UK

Polity Press
101 Station Landing
Suite 300
Medford, MA 02155, USA

ISBN-13: 978-1-5095-6452-1 (hardback)
ISBN-13: 978-1-5095-6453-8 (paperback)

A catalogue record for this book is available from the British Library.

Library of Congress Control Number: 2023952088

Typeset in 11 on 14 Warnock Pro
by Cheshire Typesetting Ltd, Cuddington, Cheshire
Printed and bound in Great Britain by TJ Books Ltd, Padstow, Cornwall

The publisher has used its best endeavors to ensure that the URLs for external websites referred to in this book are correct and active at the time of going to press. However, the publisher has no responsibility for the websites and can make no guarantee that a site will remain live or that the content is or will remain appropriate.

Every effort has been made to trace all copyright holders, but if any have been overlooked the publisher will be pleased to include any necessary credits in any subsequent reprint or edition.

For further information on Polity, visit our website:
politybooks.com

You Can't Teach That!

Contents

Acknowledgments

My thanks for the helpful comments from Donald Downs, Matthew Finkin, Howard Gillman, Frank Michelman, Robert Post, David Rabban, and Timothy Zick, the kind words of encouragement from Richard Delgado and Nadine Strossen, and the research assistance of Jo Wilson.

I am grateful to Karen Gantz and Louise Knight for their support of this project and their efficiency in seeing it through to completion.

An earlier version of parts of this argument appeared in the *Wake Forest Law Review*, and material from that article is reproduced here with the journal's permission.

Introduction

Public confidence in American universities is in freefall, especially among more conservative citizens. Politicians have taken notice and have taken aim at everything that they think might be wrong on campus. Universities are said to have gone "woke." Professors are denounced for trying to indoctrinate their students. University classrooms are thought to be filled with dangerous ideas like critical race theory. Red-state legislatures from Ohio to Florida to Texas have taken what were once thought to be radical reform ideas and moved them into the mainstream. Florida Governor Ron DeSantis has declared that "we will not let the far-left woke agenda take over our schools," and the Stop WOKE Act became one of his signature pieces of legislation. Not content with that, however, he went back to his state legislature for more. Other Republican leaders have raced to make sure that they are not outflanked on this issue.

Conservatives have complained for decades about tenured radicals and political correctness on college campuses, but the willingness of politicians to do something about those complaints is a new and extraordinary development. We are at the beginning of a debate that could reshape the landscape of higher education in America.

This book guides the general reader, students, and leaders in higher education through the difficult challenges that this new movement poses to the way things have been done, and it mounts an argument that policies like the Stop WOKE Act violate the First Amendment and that the Constitution puts meaningful constraints on the power of politicians to dictate what is taught in university classrooms. Universities are on the frontlines of the new culture war, and we should understand the significance of what that means.

The book does not argue the pros and cons of critical race theory. I am on the political right myself, and I have my own concerns with the substance of those ideas. Moreover, critical race theory is only the target *du jour*. The public rhetoric about critical race theory does not always track well the contours of the scholarly literature in critical race theory, and the policies actually adopted do not reference critical race theory as such. From a constitutional perspective, the details of the ideas and viewpoints being suppressed do not matter. If legislatures can restrict the teaching of "critical race theory" in state university classrooms today, they can equally restrict the discussion of any number of ideas, from evolutionary theory to constitutional originalism to transgenderism to settler colonialism, tomorrow.

Likewise, I take for granted the proposition that traditional notions of academic freedom are worth defending in the current moment. That is an increasingly controversial assumption, with many on the political right starting to doubt that universities are worth preserving in their current form. Despite my worries about the state of academia, I remain optimistic about its future and believe that high-quality scholarly institutions can only be built on the foundation of robust protections for academic freedom. Ultimately, academic freedom helps protect the scholarly free inquiry that generates new and important insights and intellectual breakthroughs.

My concern in this book is with censorship and the extent to which government officials can suppress ideas that they find disturbing. Are state universities at the mercy of politicians, or are there limits to what government officials can do when they do not like what university professors are saying or teaching?

This book lays out the case for why laws like the Stop WOKE Act pose a nearly unprecedented assault on American higher education and raise deep First Amendment concerns. Scholars and commentators have spent little time thinking about who controls the classrooms in state universities. For decades public universities have been left largely to their own devices. Those days are over. Politicians have pledged that they are going to clean house and rein in radical professors. Whether they successfully do that will have lasting consequences for the future of American universities and for the divide between private and public universities and between so-called red and blue states.

The book offers an argument that the First Amendment limits the ability of politicians to suppress controversial ideas in universities. It does not call for an entirely new First Amendment jurisprudence but argues that our current understandings of the First Amendment can be sufficient to the task if we take the time to understand how they should apply in a university context. We should recognize, however, that it is far from obvious the courts would or should step in to constrain government officials who want to exclude what they regard as dangerous ideas from state university classrooms. I believe that recognizing such limits is the proper implication of what the Court has said in the past about the importance of free thought in American higher education, but the issues raised by current trends in the state legislatures are both novel and complex. In this book, I hope both to provide a reliable guide to those challenges and to advocate on behalf of a particular solution to them.

The book begins by overviewing the current controversies and policies that are now on the political agenda. It tells the story of how professors in the early twentieth century came to win some independence over what and how they taught in the United States. It recounts how those newly won gains came under pressure during the early days of the Cold War and how the government's desire to root out radicals put universities in the political crosshairs. The U.S. Supreme Court responded to those Cold War controversies by declaring that academic freedom was protected to some degree by the First Amendment, but the Court did not provide any real guidance as to what degree that might be the case or how it was supposed to work.

With that background in view, we can turn to current controversies and how existing judicial doctrine regarding the First Amendment can impose some limits on how politicians can interfere in the scholarly and educational activities of universities. Despite the fact that state university professors are government employees, and that the government can engage in its own speech to convey its favored messages, politicians cannot necessarily commandeer state university classrooms and dictate what professors say in them. The Constitution provides more room for government officials to restrain professors from engaging in indoctrination in the classroom, but here too there are substantial constitutional and practical difficulties.

We are at the beginning of a potentially far-reaching reconsideration of the role of universities in American life and of the authority of politicians to take action against controversial ideas being taught and discussed on college campuses. These efforts will test the willingness of courts to defend professors and universities from political interventions and challenge our understanding of how the First Amendment applies to university classrooms. Potentially at stake is whether American universities will continue to be some of the preeminent institutions of scholarly research and of higher education in the world.

1

The Culture War and the Universities

On December 15, 2021, Florida Governor Ron DeSantis announced a new education initiative before an enthusiastic crowd at an "active adult retirement community" in Central Florida. "Nobody wants this crap. Okay? This is an elite-driven phenomenon being driven by bureaucratic elites, elites in universities and elites in corporate America. And they're trying to shove it down the throats of the American people. You're not doing that in the state of Florida."[1] The crap in question was "critical race theory," and the governor assured his supporters that Floridians were not going to take it.

With Donald Trump out of the White House, the Florida Republican was not only ramping up for his own reelection in 2022 but also eyeing a bigger prize in 2024. Much of his first term had been consumed by the COVID-19 pandemic, and DeSantis had become a GOP favorite by declaring his state open for business soon after the rollout of a vaccine and when the president and many other big-state governors were still embracing a more restrictionist approach.

Searching for a new issue that would keep him in the limelight, he quickly settled on education. He was not alone in doing so. Other Republican politicians were seeing the same political opportunities. Education provided a policy issue that allowed Republican state politicians simultaneously to put more separation between themselves and their blue state peers and to touch on multiple concerns of conservative activists and voters.

"In Florida we are taking a stand against the state-sanctioned racism that is critical race theory," DeSantis declared. ""We won't allow Florida tax dollars to be spent teaching kids to hate our country or to hate each other. We also have a responsibility to ensure that parents have the means to vindicate their rights when it comes to enforcing state standards." As he moved more educational policies toward adoption, DeSantis added, "It used to be thought that a university campus was a place where you would be exposed to a lot of different ideas. Unfortunately, now the norm is really, these are more intellectually repressive environments. You have orthodoxies that are promoted and other viewpoints are shunned, or even suppressed. We don't want that in Florida." "We obviously want our universities to be focused on critical thinking, academic rigor. We do not want them as basically hotbeds for stale ideology. That's not worth tax dollars and it's not something that we will be supporting."[2]

DeSantis was neither the first nor the last Republican politician to set his sights on the universities. When former Vice President Mike Pence chose to reenter the political arena, a major – and perhaps most quoted – component of his first speech focused on the problem of American universities.

> We will reject critical race theory in our schools, in our public universities, and we will cancel cancel culture wherever it arises. That's an agenda that'll win. That's an agenda that'll win back America. And it's a positive agenda in these divided times that each and every one of us needs to take to our neighbors and friends. We've all been through a lot over the past year. A global pandemic, civil unrest, divisive election, tragedy at our

nation's capital, and a new administration attempt on further dividing our country as they advance the agenda of the radical Left.

"Critical race theory is," Pence later asserted, "state-sanctioned racism."[3]

A new conservative advocacy group urged politicians to pledge themselves to "restore honest, patriotic education that cultivates in our children a profound love for our country." Republican politicians scrambled to sign on. Initially focused on K-12 education, the ambitions of the group – and the scope of the pledge – soon grew to include universities. Voters were urged to work to replace everyone from school board members to deans and university presidents "who promote a false, divisive, and radical view of America and our fellow citizens."[4]

Dan Patrick, the powerful Texas lieutenant governor, found himself in a war of words with members of the state university faculty over the teaching of critical race theory. After the state legislature adopted a ban on critical race theory in primary and secondary schools, the Faculty Council at the University of Texas adopted a resolution declaring that it "rejects any attempts by bodies external to the faculty to restrict or dictate the content of university curriculum on any matter, including matters related to racial and social justice." Patrick, who was in the midst of a Republican primary campaign himself, did not let the opportunity pass. "We are not going to allow a handful of professors who do not represent the entire group to teach, and indoctrinate, students with critical race theory that we are inherently racist as a nation." "To these professors . . . telling taxpayers, and the parents and the legislature and your own Board of Regents to get out of their business (and) that we have no say in what you do in the classroom, you've opened the door for this issue because you went too far, and we're going to take this on. It'll be a top priority." For good measure, he announced "Tenure, it's time that comes to an end in Texas."

Patrick was good to his word in getting bills on both issues through the Senate, where the lieutenant governor serves as presiding officer, though they were narrowly defeated in the lower chamber in 2023.[5]

The culture war was coming to campus. In hindsight, it is remarkable that it took so long.

Of course, college campuses were not exactly new to the culture war. They had long been a prime battleground, and echoes of those earlier campus battles were now resonating across the country and coming back around to the universities. State political leaders might have just been joining the battle, but right-wing activists had been in the trenches for years. A young William F. Buckley broke onto the postwar national scene with a diatribe aimed at his alma mater, Yale University. As he was organizing the modern conservative movement at mid-century, he did not forget higher education and helped put together a new student group, Young Americans for Freedom, to carry the conservative movement onto the campuses. Where Buckley focused his complaint about academia on how religion and economics were treated on campus, a young Dinesh D'Souza made his own leap onto the national stage shortly after the Berlin Wall came down with a jeremiad aimed at race and sex on campus, anticipating and reflecting the shift of conservative attention from the Cold War to the culture war. In the years after the Vietnam War, leftists joked about the pressure in their ranks to be "politically correct." By the end of Ronald Reagan's presidency in the 1980s, conservatives had taken to denouncing universities for enforcing an orthodoxy of political correctness. President George H.W. Bush even featured, to audience applause, that concern in a commencement address at the University of Michigan, denouncing the growing intolerance on university campuses to the freedom "to think and speak one's mind." During the presidency of Barack Obama, activists succeeded in popularizing "get woke" as a call to arms for social justice. By the end of the presidency of

Donald Trump, conservative activists had repurposed "woke" into a term of condemnation, with special application to the denizens of American universities. As Obama was leaving the White House, the conservative advocacy group Turning Point USA launched the Professor Watchlist to spotlight professors who advocate "anti-American values." The Marxist-turned-conservative activist David Horowitz had anticipated the Watchlist years before with his own list of the "most dangerous academics in America." There has been a seemingly insatiable appetite on the right for sensationalistic stories about American college campuses, feeding a steady stream of books and media coverage on the failings of universities.

Despite such long-standing conservative complaints about tenured radicals, universities mostly escaped much political scrutiny. There was a significant gap between how conservatives reacted to the individual stories about political correctness on college campuses and how they felt about higher education as a whole. A populist wave changed all that.

It probably did not help that the horror stories coming out of academia no longer take the form of descriptions on the page. Conservatives living far away from college campuses could now see the political excesses with their own eyes. When American Enterprise Institute scholar Charles Murray got shouted down at Middlebury College in the spring of 2017, conservatives in the Midwest got to see the whole drama play itself out on video. Something that once might have been a brief topic of conversation on campus and in the AEI buffet line could now be watched and replayed on any computer screen and support extended coverage and dissection in conservative media. Worse yet, the Middlebury incident proved not to be unique, and videos of similar events piled up. Meanwhile, social media brought the unvarnished political views of professors across the country into the open. The most outrageous examples are helpfully curated by conservative activists and distributed to a vast, eager audience.

The confluence of the new information environment and the populist takeover of Republican politics has had dire consequences for American higher education. In 2015, nearly sixty percent of respondents told Gallup that they had a great deal or quite a lot of confidence in higher education. Eight years later that number had flipped, and more respondents indicated that they had very little confidence in higher education than said that they had a great deal of confidence. The drop was particularly dramatic among self-identified Republicans, but independents were not far behind.[6] Perhaps even more dramatic were the findings of a Pew poll in 2019 that a solid majority of Republicans thought universities have a "negative effect on the way things are going in the country."[7]

Such dismal approval numbers have made American universities politically vulnerable as they rarely have been before. For a time, the more treacherous political environment expressed itself in bills demanding greater protections for free speech on campus and an openness to imposing new taxes on the largest of university endowments. The fallout from the killing of George Floyd by police officers in Minneapolis just two months after the beginning of the pandemic lockdown in the spring of 2020 created a new focal point for critics of the universities. Ideas that had once flown under the radar suddenly were on full display, from calls to defund the police and abolish prisons to demands for racial reparations. At the same time Nikole Hannah-Jones was awarded a Pulitzer Prize for her controversial collection of essays on race in American history in the *New York Times*. A conservative backlash to progressive ideas about race was brewing, and schools became the battle ground.

The Ban on "Critical Race Theory"

With remarkable speed, policymakers across the country have focused their attention on what is sometimes characterized as "divisive concepts." President Donald Trump got the ball rolling when he issued an executive order at the beginning of the 2020 electoral campaign season, seeking to root out "divisive concepts" in the federal government. His executive order identified a list of concepts, including such claims as that the "United States is fundamentally racist" and that "any individual should feel discomfort, guilt, anguish, or any form of psychological distress on account of his or her race or sex," that should be purged from federal employee training.[8] That executive order was immediately rescinded by President Joe Biden after his inauguration in early 2021, but it laid the groundwork for a great deal of policymaking to come.

Trump's executive order could in turn be traced to the efforts of Christopher Rufo. A fellow at the Manhattan Institute, a conservative think tank based in New York City, Rufo published a piece in the think tank's journal that caught the attention of the White House. Published shortly after police and Black Lives Matter protestors clashed just outside the White House fence, the short article called attention to the rise of "profiteering race theorists" peddling "white fragility" to the federal bureaucracy. Rufo had received leaked documents from workplace training sessions in the Treasury Department, which instructed federal employees that "virtually all White people contribute to racism" and do not "support the dismantling of racist institutions." White employees were told that they should "sit in the discomfort" of their own racism and should grin and bear it "if a person of color 'responds to their oppression in a way [they] don't like.'" Rufo revealed that millions of federal dollars had already been spent on such training sessions and called for conservatives to "brace for a long war against the diversity–industrial complex and its enablers."[9]

The piece foreshadowed what soon became a staple of Rufo's writing, the acquisition and publication of diversity training documents from schools and workplaces across the country. He became the self-appointed voice of disgruntled white-collar workers everywhere.

Almost as an afterthought, Rufo's article attributed the ideas that permeated diversity training to critical race theory, which he characterized as "the academic discourse centered on the concepts of 'whiteness,' 'white fragility,' and 'white privilege.'" The diversity–industrial complex was "the ultimate vision of critical race theorists" and its goal of creating "a new, radical political consciousness." Among his proposals was an executive order banning the teaching of "the toxic principles of critical race theory, race essentialism, and neo-segregationism."

Infamously, Rufo laid out his rhetorical strategy in public via Twitter: "The goal is to have the public read something crazy in the newspaper and immediately think 'critical race theory.'" He declared success in freezing their brand "into the public conversation" and "steadily driving up negative perceptions. We will eventually turn it toxic, as we put all of the various cultural insanities under that brand category."[10] The plan seems to have worked. Lots of things were soon lumped under the label, and "critical race theory" became a catch-all, if dimly understood, way for conservatives to describe racial ideas and arguments that they did not like.

Rufo was hardly alone in trying to freeze the brand. James Lindsay, a mathematician turned conservative cultural critic, was working the same beat. Lindsay had made a name for himself by contributing to a set of hoax academic papers designed to show the intellectual weakness of so-called "grievance studies." He helped bring "woke" into the conservative lexicon and explored critical race theory in depth. Central to Lindsay's charge was that critical race theory was not merely a scholarly enterprise but was a political movement pressed by a coalition of scholars and activists. What was more, critical race theorists were "totalitarians" who did not simply seek to understand the world but "*to change it*, to reorganize it according to social power dynamics it obsesses over but can only barely understand." Critical race theory was, at heart, "a *Marxian* Theory."[11] The Cold War met the cultural war.

Soon Republican legislators across the country were rushing to introduce bills that were similarly aimed at "critical race theory" and "divisive concepts" in state government. Unlike Trump's executive order, however, many of these state-level bills were aimed at educational institutions. The first wave of bills generally focused on primary and secondary schools. Arizona prohibited state agencies from making use of employee training that "presents any form of blame or judgment on the basis of race, ethnicity, or sex."[12] Georgia adopted the Protect Students First Act, which prohibited "classroom instruction" that "advocate[s] for divisive concepts," including that individuals should "feel anguish" or "guilt" "by virtue of his or her race" and that "character traits such as a hard work ethic are racist."[13] North Dakota required that the public-school curriculum be "factual" and "objective" and "not include instruction relating to critical race theory."[14] South Carolina included a budget rider on "partisanship curriculum" that prohibited curricula, textbooks, or instructional materials that "serve to inculcate" various disfavored concepts.[15] Texas adopted a civics training program that included a prohibited list of divisive concepts.[16] The list goes on.

A second wave took aim at higher education. As state politicians looked toward state universities and colleges, they also began to move forward a broader set of higher education reforms ranging from modifying faculty tenure policies to banning the use of diversity statements in university admissions and hiring to dismantling offices of diversity, equity, and inclusion. Although there are policy arguments to be had about the wisdom of this wider array of legislative initiatives, the proposals aimed at university classroom teaching are particularly significant for how universities operate and raise distinctive constitutional challenges.

Perhaps the most high-profile of the bills that have been signed into law is Florida's so-called "Stop WOKE Act," or House Bill 7. Passed with great fanfare at the behest of the governor's office, Florida Republican governor Ron DeSantis declared that "we will not let the far-left woke agenda take over our schools" and that "there is no place for indoctrination" in the state.[17] A key feature of the law echoes other "divisive concepts" proposals. It declares it to be prohibited "discrimination on the basis of race" for any student in the state to be exposed to "training or instruction that espouses, promotes, advances, inculcates, or compels such students . . . to believe any" of a list of concepts, including that members of one race are "morally superior" to members of another, that a person's "status" is "either privileged or oppressed" as a result of their race or sex, that a person "should be discriminated against or receive adverse treatment to achieve diversity, equity, or inclusion," or that "such virtues as merit, excellence, hard work, fairness, objectivity, and racial colorblindness are racist or sexist."[18] By prohibiting university instruction that "espouses," "promotes," or "advances," or offers with "endorsement" such concepts, the state restricts ordinary academic discourse in a range of disciplines and hampers the ability of professors to construct ordinary political and policy arguments relating to a variety of disputed issues involving race and sex.[19]

The policy agenda regarding the discussion of controversial ideas in public universities is mutating rapidly. New targets for regulation have quickly emerged, and policymakers have considered an array of regulatory tools. Interestingly, the Manhattan Institute itself has shied away from advising legislators to restrict teaching in state university classrooms. In urging regulation of primary and secondary schools, the Institution cautioned that the "legal parameters governing

how state elected officials interact with public university curricular decisions are very different from the K-12 context."[20]
Other advocates have not been so hesitant, and legislators
have rushed to fill the legislative hopper with anti-critical race
theory bills. Hundreds of separate proposals were introduced
just in the first two years of the Biden administration, with a
high success rate of getting adopted in some form. A significant fraction of those measures targeted higher education.[21]

If Florida's Stop WOKE Act takes a broad approach to
restricting the advocacy of divisive concepts in state university classrooms, Idaho's statute takes a narrower approach. It
makes direct reference to "tenets . . . often found in 'critical
race theory'" in its new legislation on "dignity and nondiscrim-
ination in public education." Because the legislature regards
such concepts as likely to "exacerbate and inflame divisions,"
it prohibits any "public institution of higher education" from
directing or compelling students "to personally affirm, adopt,
or adhere to" a list of tenets, including that a race or sex is inherently superior to another, that individuals should be adversely
treated on the basis of such characteristics, or that individuals
are "inherently responsible" for actions committed in the past
by other individuals who share such characteristics.[22]

Other proposals are even more ambitious. Some would ban
universities from using Nikole Hannah-Jones's 1619 Project in
university courses. Others would prohibit university professors from "teaching" disfavored ideas or using any instructional
materials discussing such ideas. Some would expand the set of
divisive concepts that could not be promoted in a university
classroom, such as the idea that capitalism or free markets
are racist. It is not hard to imagine a further expansion of
the list of forbidden divisive concepts to include such newly
salient ideas as "intersectionality," "decolonization," or "settler
colonialism." If classroom discussions and classroom materials
are to be regulated, it would not be hard to imagine policymakers turning their attention to the scholarship produced by

state university faculty or their personal political activities and speech. Dan Patrick warned controversial professors to look for employment elsewhere. "Go to a private school, let them raise their own funds to teach, but we're not going to fund them. I'm not going to pay for that nonsense."[23] If professors spouting "nonsense" is a good reason for government officials to get rid of them, it seems unlikely that the only nonsense that will matter is that being expressed in the classroom.

Can You Teach That?

Dan Patrick was flabbergasted by the implications of the resolution adopted by the University of Texas faculty. "They don't understand that we in the legislature represent the people of Texas. We are those who distribute taxpayer dollars. We are the ones who pay their salaries, parents are the ones who pay tuition. Of course, we're going to have a say in what the curriculum is."[24]

Rufo reaches a similar conclusion by a somewhat different path. He rejects what he calls the "old right-libertarian solutions." Better to rethink the relationship between public universities and the state. "I believe that we must revive the democratic governance of our public universities and shape them according to the principles and priorities of voters, who elect legislators to govern state institutions in the interest of the common good." The old "norms of academic freedom" no longer work. It is time to "engage in a strategy of political recapture." In his view, the university faculty have "broken your end of the bargain; now we're going to bring accountability." It is the democratically elected representatives of the state who should and do have the ultimate authority to determine what happens in state university classrooms. "This is not a free marketplace of ideas; this is a state-run monopoly on education institutions. And we have a duty and responsibility to use political power to shape them towards serving the citizen, towards serving the public good."[25]

The vision of state higher education advanced by politicians like DeSantis and Patrick and activists like Rufo is gaining ground and finding its way into public policy. This book examines whether there are any constitutional limitations on whether and how that vision can be put into practice. If the legislature pays the bill (though notably a much smaller portion of the bill than once was the case), does it ultimately get to call the tune of what ideas are professed in the classroom? If public universities are instruments of the state, to what extent can legislatures direct what is taught in those state agencies?

The constitutional answer to such questions is far from clear when it comes to state universities, and it is the task of this book to try to clarify that answer. The constitutional answer is already fairly clear in two other contexts, and so it is worth calling attention to them in order to set them aside. First, public primary and secondary schools have long been recognized as being under the direct political control of public bodies, from local school boards to state government officials. Teachers in the classroom at the K-12 level are agents of the state, and they are expected to teach the publicly approved curriculum. To date the courts have recognized no meaningful First Amendment rights on the part of primary and secondary-school teachers to resist legislative restrictions on their classroom speech. The initial wave of legislation targeting primary and secondary schools may be badly written and vague in ways that are constitutionally problematic, but the basic authority of the state to control what happens in public schools is expansive. Second, private universities are largely beyond the control of the state governments. Private educational institutions have substantial First Amendment rights to design and teach their own curriculum without state interference. The constitutional space for government officials to attempt to restrict what is taught in private university classrooms is exceedingly limited. Constitutionally speaking, the University of Texas is situated very differently from Princeton University. There is relatively little politicians could do to gag professors at Princeton University or any other private university. It is much less clear what they can constitutionally do to gag professors at the University of Texas or any other public university.

In the following pages, I make out the argument that there are meaningful constitutional limitations on the authority of legislatures to restrict what ideas are discussed and how they are discussed in public university classrooms – at least as those universities are currently constituted.

Broadly speaking, legislative proposals to restrict the teaching of divisive concepts in state university classrooms have taken two forms. One would prohibit professors from advocating or promoting the forbidden ideas. A second would prohibit professors from attempting to compel students to believe such ideas. Both types are constitutionally fraught, though the first is more obviously so than the second. Both types attempt to identify what is politically heterodox and drive it out of state universities.

Each type is considered in turn. Chapters 5 and 6 examine the constitutional concerns raised by policies banning the promotion of disfavored ideas in state university classrooms. They conclude that state university professors should be understood to enjoy some degree of autonomy in determining what ideas they discuss in the classroom and how those ideas are presented. To be sure, that autonomy is not without limits. Academic freedom exists to protect the ability of academics to conduct their duties in a professionally appropriate manner and not in whatever manner politicians or donors might prefer. The recognition of a First Amendment interest in academic freedom is meant to purify the scholarly enterprise, but a precondition of that recognition is the understanding that professors will adhere to that scholarly enterprise and not corrupt that mission or abuse the freedom that they have been given.

Chapter 7 takes up the more complicated task of determining what a ban on compelling belief in the classroom might entail. Such policies tap into intuitive ideas that students also enjoy First Amendment rights in a state university classroom and that professors should not use their authority to inappropriately coerce students into embracing the professors' ideas. Determining what is inappropriate in this context is a subtle task. Even so, such policy proposals are not content to protect students from attempted indoctrination. They take aim not at unprofessional conduct in the classroom but at the introduction of politically disfavored ideas into the classroom. To the extent that such policies have any meaningful effect at all, they will serve to discourage professors from broaching subjects that politicians would prefer not to see discussed.

2

Academic Freedom in the United States

As part of its commencement celebrations in May of 1878, Vanderbilt University in Nashville, Tennessee, had scheduled a public lecture by one of its distinguished professors. Formerly a professor at the University of Michigan and the chancellor of Syracuse University, Alexander Winchell had been recruited to the newly established Vanderbilt University to teach geology and zoology. The subject of his address was to be "Man in the Light of Geology."

Students had only arrived on the new campus in the fall of 1875. The southern denomination of the Methodist church had planned to found a new university in Tennessee, but those plans were shelved during the Civil War and Reconstruction. Surprisingly, the shipping magnate Cornelius Vanderbilt took an interest in the project and provided the funds to launch the new endeavor, and the builders quickly broke ground for a university that would bear its benefactor's name.

Vanderbilt opened its doors at a transition point in American higher education. Most universities in the United States had begun with strong ties to a church, and training ministers was often the primary mission. In the years after the Civil War, the college landscape began to change. Aided by federal land grants, state universities were springing up across the country with a goal of educating a broader class of Americans and providing useful knowledge to fuel the American economy. Even the older colleges began to make space for teaching in the natural sciences. Harvard University had just appointed a chemist to be its president, and Charles Eliot embarked on an ambitious project of converting Harvard into a serious research university. The year after students first enrolled in Vanderbilt, Johns Hopkins launched with the explicit aim of being a secular research university like the leading institutions of Europe. Although under the sponsorship of the Methodist church, Vanderbilt did not follow the old convention of choosing a minister to administer the university. Instead, the board turned to Landon Garland, a physics and geology professor with experience running a university. Active in the Methodist church, Garland had helped stymie an earlier proposal to establish a theology school, arguing instead that what was needed was a first-rate university with a department of biblical studies, sitting alongside departments of science, medicine, and law. Recruiting serious scholars from the North like Winchell signaled that Vanderbilt University meant to be truly national in spirit and to establish its place as a leading American university.

Winchell was a celebrated figure and a popular lecturer, but the invitation to speak at commencement was not a mere honorific. It turned out to be an ambush. Some months before, Winchell had given a public lecture back in Syracuse, New York. The local Nashville paper carried a report of this "interesting lecture" on "the origin of the races." Winchell boldly told his New York audience, "New truths are better than old errors." While we should mourn "the loss of a belief," "it is only truth which is divine." The Syracuse lecture previewed Winchell's latest scholarly tract, an examination of the prehistoric origins of mankind. He contended that the scientific evidence demonstrated that the "first of all men . . . appeared in Africa" and were blessed with "the divine spark of intelligence." They were, Winchell thought, "pre-Adamites" and the natural ancestors of the modern inhabitants of Africa. The Adam of the Bible was created later and elsewhere, and from him modern Europeans descended. Winchell declined to say whether the first men were "descended from a being unworthy to be called a man," but insisted that the diversity of humankind and "the epoch of his first appearance on the earth" were "subjects to be settled by scientific investigation." Religious faith, he warned, should not be tied to "corruptible science." Science advanced through theory and evidence, and scientific opinion could "vanish like a summer cloud" in the face of new theories and better evidence. Winchell's own theory of the origin of the races could be right or wrong (in fact, his theory was idiosyncratic even in his own time), but his argument would be judged by the scientific method and not biblical exegesis. Religious believers should learn "to discriminate between religious faiths and scientific opinions."[1]

Less than an hour before he was to deliver his commencement speech at Vanderbilt, Winchell met with the chair of the board of trustees, Bishop Holland McTyeire. McTyeire was not there simply to exchange pleasantries. As the professor later recounted, the bishop "embraced the opportunity to introduce a business which caused me extraordinary surprise." The bishop wanted to inform him that "we are having considerable annoyance from the criticisms which are passed by our people on some of your positions in matters of opinion, and it is likely to increase." To put it bluntly, "they object to evolution." Winchell protested that he had never publicly endorsed the theory of human evolution, but the chairman of the board was not there to argue with him. It was enough that "our people are complaining, and the University will suffer." The board was giving the professor an opportunity to "relieve us of our embarrassments," and it would be meeting right after Winchell's commencement address. Indeed it had been the bishop who had suggested that Winchell's commencement address be on subject of evolution. The professor had not appreciated the significance of that suggestion, and now the bishop wished to make it plain. "I wanted you to have an opportunity to put yourself right."

Winchell was given a choice. He could either use his commencement address explicitly to renounce the theory of evolution or he could resign his professorship. Winchell refused either option. "If the Board have the manliness to dismiss me for cause, and declare the cause, I prefer they should do it." If they took that step, Winchell vowed, it would be "unjust and oppressive, as well as discrediting to the University. It will recoil upon its authors." The board, McTyeire rejoined, did not "propose to treat you as the Inquisition treated Galileo," but Winchell insisted "what you propose is the same thing." "It is ecclesiastical proscription for an opinion which *must be settled by scientific evidence.*"[2] The next day Winchell received his notice of termination.

Winchell did not go quietly. Unlike many younger and less well-established professors, he was willing to stake his reputation against that of the fledgling Vanderbilt University. He took his case to the press and rallied his allies to his defense. Although Winchell declared that he had always striven to avoid "any utterance offensive to strait orthodoxy," he also insisted that universities would engage in a "gross perversion of a sacred trust" if professors "are forbidden to proclaim principles of science which have gained almost universal acceptance."[3] Winchell might have thought himself secure in his position at Vanderbilt since he had, as his defenders in the press noted, taken on the "thankless office of a reconciler between theology and science" and had offered up "so conservative a presentation of the race question" that his Southern white neighbors should not have objected.[4]

If so, he miscalculated. The Darwinist *Popular Science Monthly* fulminated, "Vanderbilt fought the progress of science by bigotry, intolerance and proscription." The *Nashville Christian Advocate* retorted,

> The people – "our people" – have no objection to orthodoxy. Parents who have sons to be educated prefer the safety of that atmosphere to genteel infidelity. Let anti-Methodist critics rage – Vanderbilt University is safe. . . . Those who are in charge of it know what they are about.[5]

Vanderbilt had, according to the *Atlanta Daily Constitution*, merely "asserted the right of self-protection, the right of self-control, the right of self-direction – nothing else." The university, "because of him, was inevitably doomed to be identified with 'advanced' scientific theories," and the board of trustees appropriately recognized that it had a higher duty "to guard its students against all scientific scepticism."[6] The quarrelsome professor was sent back to Ann Arbor.

The battle over Darwinism was not unique to Vanderbilt, and the Winchell affair was neither the first nor the last skirmish. Shortly after Winchell left Tennessee, the famed sociologist William Graham Sumner found himself in a fight with the president of Yale College. Perhaps the nation's pre-mier "Social Darwinist," Sumner assigned as a coursebook a text by the English writer Herbert Spencer. Spencer applied evolutionary theory and the mantra of "survival of the fittest" to the social world rather than the natural world. President Noah Porter did not object to the teaching of Charles Darwin in the natural sciences at Yale. He had strong views, however, about the "so-called science" of sociology. He viewed Spencer and other upstart social scientists as teaching a "theology" in disguise, and one very much at odds with the teachings of the Bible. In Porter's view, Spencer should only be introduced into a Yale classroom in order to be denounced. That was certainly not Sumner's plan. Although much of their dispute played out behind closed doors, it too attracted newspaper coverage with the *New York Times* breathlessly telling readers that the fight between Porter and Sumner "involves the whole issue between science and religion, and its final settlement will decide the attitude of the college toward the modern spirit of inquiry, which proposes to be guided by reason rather than by faith."[7]

Perhaps less momentously it was a battle over whether a university president or a university professor controlled the books that could be assigned in university classrooms, and whether the emerging social sciences would enjoy the same autonomy and respect as the natural sciences. Sumner posited that his duty as a professor was to "bend all my efforts to study and teach political and social science according to the advance of sound learning in regard to those matters," and he had "supposed that I was just as free as any other professor" to explore the ideas in his chosen discipline. Sumner placed an ultimatum before the board of trustees: "It is impossible . . . for me to submit to interference with my work." If the university was prepared to discipline him for being "indiscreet, silly, negligent, incompetent, immoral, or otherwise unfit for his position," then it should do so. If Yale was not prepared to take that step, then it should put an end to the controversy and let Sumner get back to work.[8] In the end, both sides backed away from the brink. Porter ceased meddling with Sumner's classes, and Sumner refrained from teaching a class in sociology for a few years. At Yale, at least, the question of who decided what could be taught in a university classroom was put off for a bit longer.

Not long thereafter, James Woodrow was drummed out of the Columbia Theological Seminary in South Carolina. Woodrow was an uncle of Woodrow Wilson, and, like his nephew, he was among a new wave of American scholars who had travelled to Germany to earn a Ph.D. Those European-trained professors brought back to America not only cutting-edge learning in their particular scholarly disciplines but also new ideas about academic freedom. In addition to his advanced schooling in the natural sciences, Woodrow was also a trained minister, and he was recruited to the seminary to help train "men capable of defending the faith" in "an age in which the most insidious attacks are made upon revealed religion, through the natural sciences." Woodrow arrived at the seminary declaring that he saw his task as one of harmonizing reason and religion and that in order to do so effectively he and his students "while thus engaged, the most untrammeled freedom of inquiry must be allowed."[9] In time the governors there likewise demanded that the professor state plainly his views on human evolution, and Woodrow obliged them by declaring that he believed that God directly supplied Adam with a soul but supplied Adam with a body only indirectly through the process of evolution. After an extended internal battle, the general assembly of the Southern Presbyterian Church resolved that Adam's body was directly created by God out "of the dust on the ground without any natural animal parentage of any kind." A decade after Winchell left Vanderbilt, Woodrow was fired from the seminary, and the seminarians were prohibited from attending any of the lectures he delivered at the nearby University of South Carolina.[10]

Nearly three decades later, the battle over the teaching of evolution raged anew. This time the battle was political and legislative. State legislatures across the country, but particularly in the South, were lobbied to adopt laws banning the teaching of evolution in public schools. In the end, most of those lobbying efforts failed, though it was often a close call. University of Kentucky President Frank McVey resolved to "fight as vigorously as possible" in his state.[11] He made an appearance in both chambers of the Kentucky legislature and released a statement directly to the people of the state. On the one hand, he sought to reassure Kentuckians that their state university did not teach "atheism, agnosticism, and Darwinism," and that "no member of the staff of the University attempts, directly or indirectly, to modify, alter, or shape the religious beliefs of students." On the other hand, he emphasized that "such legislation is exceedingly dangerous in that it places limitations on the right of thought and freedom of belief. If the history of America has stood for anything it has stood for freedom of belief, freedom of speech, and tolerance in religious matters."[12] The anti-evolution bill failed in Kentucky, but it succeeded in Tennessee. In Tennessee, observers thought "the University stood in constant terror of the legislature."[13] With anti-evolution bills under active debate, a dean at the University of Tennessee rescinded a professor's course book order that included a text applying evolutionary theory to humans and fired the professor who had sought to teach that material. Some suspected that the professor's true crime was not so much the inclusion of evolution in his class but "his unqualified insistence upon teaching it and some lack of tact in teaching it." As controversy over the firing broke into public, university offices were flooded with letters praising or condemning the actions of university officials. For some, the university deserved high praise for taking a stand "in the matter of seeing that no dangerous books are permitted at the University."[14] The Butler Act passed the Tennessee state legislature by large margins in 1925 and prohibited "any teacher of the Universities, Normals, and all other public schools of the State that are supported in whole or in part by the public school funds of the State" from teaching "that man has descended from a lower order of animals."[15] The Butler Act later gained infamy in the "Scopes Monkey Trial," featuring a high-school teacher rather than a university professor, but it remained on the books until 1967.

"Academic Asphyxiation"

Controversies surrounding Darwinism were only the tip of the iceberg when it came to academic freedom in the United States in the decades after the Civil War. Professors were routinely dismissed from their positions for offending students with their teaching, offending alumni and donors with their scholarship, or offending anyone with their political activities. University trustees, usually operating through the hand of the university president, felt no hesitation about getting rid of members of the university faculty who were working against the best interest of the university as the trustees understood it. If there were any differences of opinion, "the professors would have to walk the plank."[16]

At a meeting of the American Sociological Society in Princeton in 1914, the University of Wisconsin sociologist Edward A. Ross called attention to the fact that "the dismissal of professors by no means gives the clue to the frequency of the gag in academic life." It was only the few who would persist in causing trouble "until they are dismissed." Those cases might generate newspaper coverage and attract the attention of scholars locally or even nationally. "We forget the many who take their medicine and make no fuss." "Academic asphyxiation" was the real problem. The Supreme Court would later call this the "chilling effect" of the threat of speech restrictions, or what free-speech scholars now call the problem of self-censorship. For every professor who was fired for saying something controversial, there were many more who learned the lesson and kept their mouths shut. Ross knew, he said, "for many of them have come and told me with bitterness and rage of the gag that has been placed in their mouths."[17] In his "Study of American Education," the muckraking socialist writer Upton Sinclair called this the "world of 'hush.'"[18]

Ross spoke with some authority on this question, not merely because he was then the sitting president of the American Sociological Society, but because he was among what we would now term "the cancelled." Ross had only recently completed his Ph.D. in political economy at Johns Hopkins when he arrived at Stanford University in 1893. He did not shrink from jumping into the public spotlight. Like other Stanford professors, he spoke out publicly about the political issues of the day. Unlike most of his colleagues, however, he spoke out in ways that were unlikely to sit well with the donor class. In the 1896 presidential elections, he supported the populist upstart William Jennings Bryan and spoke in favor of an inflationary monetary policy. He embraced a range of populist and progressive causes and, as the election season once again rolled around in 1900, he began to speak and write publicly to advance his favored political causes. Of particular significance, he called for the restriction on immigration from China and for government ownership of public utilities. Both positions ran contrary to the personal financial interests of Jane Leland Stanford, whose wealth was built on railroad and streetcar interests. Mrs. Stanford promptly informed the president of the university that "I am weary of Professor Ross, and I think he ought not be retained at Stanford University." Although the president tried to reassure Stanford that Ross was not actually a socialist and could still be useful to the university, she would not be swayed. Ross was given his walking papers, and the professor immediately called a press conference. The events at Stanford became national news, and Ross became an academic celebrity. Battle lines were drawn at Stanford, and professors resigned in protest of Stanford's actions.

The Ross affair was something of a turning point. It was not that what happened to Ross was particularly unusual, nor was Jane Stanford's attitude about the proper role of the faculty at "her" university uncommon. Ross's political opinions were not necessarily uncommon among the university faculty, but they were hardly popular among the wealthy benefactors of universities and their allies in the press and pulpit. Even some of Ross's colleagues recognized that the young professor took too much "boyish delight" in saying things that were shocking and could frequently be "unnecessarily rude and offensive," and so they were not necessarily surprised that he had gotten himself fired. The story of Ross's tumultuous tenure at Stanford was a familiar one, up to a point.

Nonetheless, the firing of Ross landed differently. Ross proved to be an adept publicist for his own cause and garnered unusually favorable and numerable press clippings, and Jane Stanford was not herself a particularly sympathetic figure.

Most notably, the academics closed ranks behind Ross. The university president had been unusually persistent in pleading his case to Jane Stanford and had sung his praises as a scholar. That paper trail became public, and it fed an emerging narrative that Stanford was letting politics and personal interest trump scholarship. Colleagues on the Stanford faculty publicly came to his defense, with one telling the press that Ross's dismissal showed the "sinister spirit of social bigotry and commercial intolerance which is just now the deadliest foe of American democracy." Stanford University was less than a decade old, and the scandal threatened to undo all the efforts that the university had made to establish itself as a serious academic enterprise. Ross was a well-known figure in the new generation of academics with advanced training and big professional ambitions. Professors from across the country were increasingly organized and in routine communication with one another. He had helped found the American Economic Association, and his fellow professionals saw his firing as a "great wrong . . . to the cause of *scientific* education and freedom of speech." As a consequence, the Association launched an unprecedented investigation of Stanford and released a scathing report. For the first time, professors at elite institutions across the country concluded, as a Harvard philosophy professor did, that "the substantial honesty of our profession is called into question," and it was essential to their professional status to demonstrate that they were not "under the sway of those powerful few, like Mrs. Stanford, who paid the bills."[19]

Just over a decade later, some of those same players began to organize a more systematic effort to develop principles and practices of academic freedom in the United States. They were not building entirely from scratch, but theirs was a radical enterprise. They were seeking to transform how American universities operated, and they were remarkably successful. Within three decades, they had remade the relationship between universities and their faculty.

"Unrestricted Research and Unfettered Discussion"

For many American academics, the German universities of the nineteenth century were held up as a model to be emulated in America. Already before the Civil War, the philosopher and first president of the University of Michigan Henry Tappan sang the praises of the German universities. They represented the ideal, of "institutions free alike from political and sectarian influence and partialities" and where "investigation and productive thought must be free as birds upon the wing."[20] By the end of the century, American education reformers were trying to import German scholarly rigor and academic freedom into the United States.

In the first decade of the twentieth century, the Carnegie Foundation for the Advancement of Teaching was launched with an aim of helping to modernize American universities. The foundation did not always imagine modernization in the same way that the professors did, but it did bemoan political meddling in American higher education. In its third annual report in 1908, it highlighted events in Oklahoma to make its point that the American people, and their political leaders, "must be educated to the idea of intellectual freedom as the atmosphere in which truth grows." The foundation fretted that so long as the people "are willing to permit the politicians to play with their highest institutions of learning, there is little hope of genuine progress." The situation in Oklahoma was especially dramatic. The Democratic Party had captured the state government for the first time, and newly elected Governor Charles Haskell promptly appointed a new board of regents, which fired the president of the University of Oklahoma and then "proceeded to investigate through a committee the professors of the university and dismissed a number, amongst them some of the best men in the institution." The newly appointed regents might be "well-meaning" and "high-minded," but in attempting to fire and replace members of the university faculty they were undertaking "a task for which they were absolutely unfit." They had dealt the university "a blow from which it will take years to recover" and sent a message to the broader academic community that the professors in that state did not enjoy the "freedom of speech and security of place" that were essential to maintaining a "true university."[21]

Meanwhile, some of the leading luminaries in the American professoriate began organizing to advocate for the kind of intellectual freedom that they thought necessary if American universities were to fulfill their promise. The formation of the American Association of University Professors (AAUP) was to provide professors with an advocacy organization for collective action to improve the lot of faculty across the country. Its initial mission was to engage in that task of educating the American people and their leaders "to the idea of intellectual freedom" and to investigate and publicize incidents in which universities failed to live up to those ideals.

The AAUP's 1915 Declaration of Principles on Academic Freedom and Tenure provided the philosophical basis for a more robust understanding of academic freedom in the United States. Some universities might simply "be used as an instrument of propaganda" by a religious sect, a political faction, or a wealthy individual and in such cases there was no point to granting academic freedom. But such institutions were also not serious educational enterprises and were of limited value to society at large. Their "purpose is not to advance knowledge by the unrestricted research and unfettered discussion of impartial investigators." They existed only to "subsidize the promotion of opinions" favored by their patrons. Real universities would instead employ real scholars "trained for, and dedicated to, the quest for truth." Their mission was not to provide "echoes of the opinions of the lay public, or of the individuals who endow or manage universities." Their mission was to advance the frontiers of human knowledge and provide society with their honest judgment and impartial expertise. In order to do that, professors would need to be granted "independence of thought and utterance" even when their ideas might prove controversial or unpopular.[22]

This idea of academic freedom was gaining ground in the United States but was a long way from being fully realized. The AAUP spent its early days exposing violations of those principles and attempting to establish a professional code of conduct that university officials would respect. The AAUP repeatedly documented efforts to suppress the controversial speech of professors. In 1915, a professor was fired from the faculty of Wharton Business School for his public support for socialist and progressive causes. In 1918, the chancellor of the University of Montana consulted the governor before ordering a professor not to publish his research on the taxation of mines in the state. In 1927, the president of the University of Louisville fired a history professor for not showing sufficient "loyalty" when the professor objected to giving academic credit to students "who had never graduated from high school, but were capable of playing football." In 1929, a professor at the University of Missouri was fired when a student in his course distributed a questionnaire to the larger student body asking about their sexual attitudes and behavior. The professor was informed that a university "must be a place to which parents may send their children with full confidence that the surrounding moral atmosphere will be sane and wholesome." The professor's teaching and research had put that in doubt. In its first years of operation, the AAUP reports were filled with dozens of such cases.[23]

Meanwhile, the AAUP worked to persuade university leaders to adopt policies protecting faculty speech. The effort bore fruit in the form of the 1940 Statement of Principles on Academic Freedom and Tenure. The 1940 Statement was jointly adopted by the American Association of University Professors and the Association of American Colleges, an organization representing a large number of university presidents. The principles laid down in that document were a bit of a compromise, but they for the first time demonstrated broad acceptance by both professors and university officials of the importance of recognizing academic freedom in American universities. The Statement stripped away the philosophical discussion that dominated the 1915 Declaration and honed in on a small number of key commitments that universities should make to their faculties. Those commitments were quickly worked into university policies and contracts throughout the country.

Academic freedom in the United States comes down to three basic propositions. These simple principles do not encompass everything that might be useful or necessary to foster a spirit of free inquiry and an active exchange of ideas. They do not guarantee that professors will be honest, unbiased, or open-minded. They do not protect professors from the pressures of social conformity or the enticements of material reward. They are, however, understood to be essential elements in constructing a university dedicated to the advancement and dissemination of human knowledge and to the provision to American society of expertise on what we know about the workings of the natural and social world.

As laid out in the 1940 Statement and incorporated into university governing documents across the country, academic freedom has three core principles.

- Teachers are entitled to full freedom in research and the publication of the results, subject to the adequate performance of their other academic duties.
- Teachers are entitled to freedom in the classroom in discussing their subject, but they should be careful not to introduce

into their teaching controversial matter that has no relation to their subject.

- College and university teachers are citizens, members of a learned profession, and officers of an educational institution. When they speak or write as citizens, they should be free from institutional censorship or discipline.[24]

Professors should enjoy freedom of research, freedom in teaching, and freedom in the expression of their personal views and opinions. It is that second freedom – the freedom of teaching – that is of immediate concern here. What are professors allowed to teach in a university classroom, and who gets to determine those limits? Within the world of American higher education, the answer is clear, even if universities do not always live up to their ideals. Professors should be allowed to teach controversial ideas that are relevant to the subject matter of their courses without the interference of those outside the faculty. What ideas are to be taught in a university classroom are not to be dictated by students, donors, university administrators, or politicians. They are to be determined by the professional judgment of the instructors.

Academic freedom, as it applies in research and teaching, is not simply a freedom of expression. In that sense, academic freedom is quite different from traditional examples of freedom of speech that are protected by the First Amendment. Academic freedom adheres to a particular professional setting, and it arises from the needs of that professional enterprise. In their teaching and scholarship, professors are not afforded a freedom to say whatever might come to mind. They are afforded the freedom to carry out their professional duties without inappropriate pressures being placed on them by their university employers. They are insulated from outside forces so that they might tell the truth as best they understand it.

The American doctrine of academic freedom is now over a century old, and it has been the mainstream commitment of

American universities since the Second World War. Academic freedom has primarily developed as a set of professional norms and contractual promises. They are designed to protect professors from reprisal by their university employer for things that they say. Universities pledged themselves to refrain from suspending, firing, or otherwise disciplining members of their faculties when they express controversial ideas that might anger or offend students, parents, donors, or politicians. Professors were not hired to say whatever local politicians or powerful businessmen might want them to say. They were hired to tell the truth as best they understood it.

3

The Era of the Loyalty Oaths

In the spring of 1935, a group of conservative students formed a chapter of the American Liberty League at the University of North Carolina with a goal of changing the university's reputation as a "hotbed of radicalism." Among their first acts was to invite David Clark to come speak at the campus.

Clark was a fitting choice for their purpose. The Liberty League was itself a new (and short-lived) organization, launched by a bipartisan but conservative group of politicians, lawyers, and businessmen to mount a public campaign in defense of private property and free enterprise. Clark was the publisher of trade journals focused on the textile industry that made up a large segment of North Carolina's economy. In that role, he had rallied Southern businessmen against liberal reform movements on issues ranging from child labor to labor unionization to school integration.

He was also a long-standing thorn in the side of the leadership of the University of North Carolina. In the 1920s, Clark had railed against the university having become "a breeding place for socialism and communism," where professors "turn aside from their duties as teachers of regular courses and seek to develop fads and fancies" with "great injury to our State."

The proper mission of a public university, Clark declared, "is to educate young men, not to reform the social and economic fabric of a state." University president Harry Chase was forced to remind angry alumni stirred up by Clark's attacks that "freedom of discussion is one of the things for which the University has always stood." Although the faculty might sometimes produce research "with whose view point as a whole there may not be general agreement," it was "only by such freedom that truth comes." But Chase balanced such defenses of academic freedom with proactive efforts to avoid excessive controversy. When a visiting fellow at the university produced a study of the wages paid by a local tobacco company to black workers, the president reported to a trustee that all copies of the manuscript "have been recalled and destroyed" along with the economist's research notes. The matter had been "cleaned up."[1]

Given a stage in a packed auditorium at the Chapel Hill campus in 1935, Clark was raring for a fight. "I condemn the cowardly attempt of certain professors to crawl under the cover of freedom of speech while trying to instill subversive doctrines into the minds of boys and girls entrusted into their care." He warned that the "University will suffer" when the state's politicians fully realized the "radical activities" that were tolerated on the campus, and he called out individual professors by name for "teaching atheism, socialism, and communism." The dean of the business school took up the challenge. He stood to ask Clark whether he could define socialism. Hoots of derision from the students rained down on Clark when he responded, "I don't know, and I don't think anybody else does." Clark was eventually forced to admit that "to some extent, yes," socialism and communism were a proper subject of study at the university. The professors Clark had called out responded in print, dismissing Clark for "parroting and insinuating things he cannot prove, the nature of which he does not understand." Clark was invited to see for himself that the professor never engages "in propaganda in my classroom."[2]

Clark was not chastened, of course, and the University of North Carolina was not the only university in the state to feel his sting. The president of the newly rechristened Duke University had to soothe the university's backers when Clark denounced it for hosting a public lecture by the socialist politician Norman Thomas. Like his counterpart at Chapel Hill, Duke President William Preston Few tried to mount a defense of intellectual freedom at the university. Few hoped that North Carolina was past the dangers "in the old South of the prostitution of higher education to politics," and he posited that "we must take the firm stand that it is the business of Duke University to hear both sides of all questions that are fairly debatable" and give the faculty "a free hand to find and proclaim the truth as they see it." Duke's trustees saw things differently. The newly installed university president did not seem to understand "the nature and extent of your responsibility" for the "mental and moral health" of the "boys and girls whose parents have committed to your care at a most impressionable age." Socialism was not the kind of thing that should be debatable on a college campus.[3]

Some years later, Clark explained to a local community group that "academic freedom is freedom to learn but not freedom to teach." After all some young students could be expected to "temporarily go off at a tangent in their thinking." They could be expected to "return to sanity" if left alone. But the students were not being left alone. Some professors were "paid to teach English" but were instead spending their time "teaching Communism." "My position is that professors and instructors, at a state-sponsored institution, should not be allowed to use their classrooms for propaganda purposes." "The radical professors shout about freedom but what they really desire is license to use a soap box in their classroom and a right to present their atheist, socialist, and communist allies to groups of students." Students could talk about what they wanted, but the professors should be kept on a tight leash.[4]

Clark's own career as a leading conservative firebrand in the South extended across a perilous time for American universities. The newly established ideal of academic freedom came under serious assault as donors and politicians worried that, as Clark explained to the Charlotte Lions Club: "it seems the credentials for permission to lecture to students have been disbelief in God, contempt for morality, disloyalty to your country and affiliation with Fifth Column efforts." Universities platformed ideas that should not be heard. They excluded those who would give voice to the ideas and values that the leaders of the community shared. They employed professors who misused their position to indoctrinate students with radical ideas. The radicals on college campuses were a "cancer" that needed to be cut out.

The First Red Scare and the Universities

The current political assault on state universities is perhaps the most substantial since the early days of the Cold War. It remains to be seen whether the current political efforts will be as consequential as those of the mid-twentieth century, but the volume and salience of political interest in speech activities on college campuses is higher now than it has been in decades. The search for "subversives" in the postwar period sought to suppress radical ideas in public and private institutions of higher education. The current wave of anti-critical race theory legislation has similar goals. The anti-subversive legislation of the Cold War era spurred the Supreme Court to begin to constitutionalize academic freedom principles. The anti-critical race theory legislation could prod the Court to push those developments further.

The original impetus for the anti-subversive push predated the Cold War.[5] The Bolshevik Revolution in Russia and the First World War generated their own demands for ensuring that subversive ideas did not get a foothold in the United States. New York had been ahead of the curve, given the flood of immigrants into New York City at the turn of the century, which brought with them a host of radical political and economic ideas. In 1902, New York had adopted a "criminal anarchy" law, which criminalized anyone who "by word of mouth or writing advocates, advises or teaches the duty, necessity or propriety of overthrowing or overturning organized government by force or violence, or by assassination . . . or by any unlawful means."[6] As America entered the First World War, states across the country followed New York's example with their own "criminal syndicalism" laws, sometimes framed as wartime measures and sometimes not. Legislators did not always confine themselves to those advocating violent revolution. West Virginia, for example, hoped to "foster the ideals, institutions and government" of the state and nation by making it unlawful "for any person to speak, print, publish, or communicate, by language, sign, picture, or otherwise, any teachings, doctrines or counsels in sympathy or favor of ideals, institutions or forms of government hostile, inimical or antagonistic to those now or hereafter existing under the constitution and laws of this state or of the United States."[7] As the First World War came to a close, the heterodox economist Thorstein Veblen wrote pleadingly, "now that the abnormal urgencies of war . . . have come to an end . . . can we look forward to something like normal conditions of freedom of speech and opinion?" Or, he feared, "is the smoke barrage of 'Bolshevism' now to be used to hide the actual suppression of honest differences of opinion and honest opposition to certain policies the [Woodrow Wilson] Administration may be pursuing?"[8] He was not optimistic.

New York took the lead again after the First World War, with a particular focus on rooting subversives out of public schools. A special joint committee of the state legislature put out a massive report in 1920 to expose the danger of "revolutionary radicalism." The report authors understood themselves to be in the midst of an ideological struggle with the proponents of Communism. "If American ideals of individual freedom and initiative are to be maintained, every citizen must be militant in their defense." A "re-education of the educators and of the educated class must go hand in hand with the reorganization and extension of our educational system." Educators were going to be at the front lines of this new kind of war, and it was essential that "they should be trained and eager to combat those [subversive] influences, and, in order that they may do this, it is essential that they themselves shall be in full accord and sympathy with our form of government and the system of society under which we live." It would no longer be enough for educators to be chosen on the basis of their academic achievements. They would also have to be examined for their "character." "Fundamentally, it is the duty of the State in the interests of its self-protection, to see that its citizens are trained to respect its laws, to revere its institutions and to accept the duties and responsibilities as well as the privileges of citizenship." The state must embrace its duty to provide "the protection of its citizens from false and subversive teaching."[9]

In the midst of radical bombings and widespread labor strife, the New York state legislature was prepared to take aggressive steps to put down the menace. It started by cleaning up its own house. Five duly elected Socialist members of the general assembly were expelled from the legislature, drawing criticism from Democratic Governor Alfred E. Smith and Republican former-governor Charles Evans Hughes. The assembly then got down to legislative business, putting forward several bills addressing the subversive threat. One bill required that each public-school teacher be certified that he is not only of good moral character but also that he "is desirous of the welfare of the country and in hearty accord and sympathy with the government and institutions of the State of New York and of the United States."[10] Governor Smith denounced the bill, saying "[i]t deprives teachers of their right to freedom of thought, it limits the teaching staff of the public schools to those only who lack the courage of mind to exercise their legal right to just criticism of existing institutions." Of another that sought to create a licensing system for private schools, he wrote, "it strikes at the very foundation of one of the most cardinal institutions of our nation – the fundamental right of the people to enjoy full liberty in the domain of idea and speech." "It is," he thought, "unthinkable that in a representative democracy there should be delegated to any body of men the absolute power to prohibit the teaching of any subject of which it may disapprove."[11] Nonetheless, when Smith left office, revised versions of the Lusk bills were adopted into law. Teachers would no longer be required to demonstrate their "hearty accord" with the government, but they would be required to prove that they had not "advocated, by word of mouth or in writing, a form of government other than the government of the United States or of this state, or who advocates or has advocated, either by word of mouth or in writing, a change in the form of government . . . by force, violence or any unlawful means."[12]

The Lusk Laws (named after their primary sponsor, Senator Clayton R. Lusk) were copied by state legislatures across the country. The Pennsylvania legislature undertook a comprehensive overhaul of the state requirements for public schools, including such details as a mandate that elementary schools "include kind treatment of horses, birds, and other animals" with their humane instruction. The state superintendent of public instruction was directed to develop "a course of instruction conducive to the spirit of loyalty and devotion to the State and National Government," consistent with a widespread effort to "Americanize" recent immigrants who often hailed from non-democratic nations.[13] Just a few years later the American Civil Liberties Union reported that "[m]ore laws interfering with the school curriculum have been passed [since the First World War] than in all the years preceding." Moreover, the

ACLU identified cases in several states in which teachers were "disciplined or silenced" even for being "politically active in opposition to the party in control" of the state government.[14]

Subversive Ideas

While the current anti-critical race theory bills have taken direct aim at university instruction, the anti-subversive efforts of the early and mid-twentieth century were generally less direct. Loyalty oaths became a condition of employment not only for teachers but for state employees of all sorts, including professors at state universities. As the country entered the Second World War, New York barred individuals "from any office or position in the service of the state" including "in a state normal school or college, or any other state educational institution" who "willfully and deliberately advocates, advises or teaches the doctrine that the government of the United States . . . should be overthrown or overturned by force, violence or any unlawful means" or becomes "a member of any society or group of persons which teaches or advocates" such a doctrine.[15] A divided Mississippi supreme court upheld the conviction of a Jehovah's Witness couple who had gone door-to-door in the summer of 1942 trying to persuade people that American participation in the war was wrong and doomed to fail. They were sentenced under a newly adopted state seditious speech statute. While the dissenting judges urged that the "freedom to hear, to think, and to teach" were central to the American experiment in free government, the majority of that court, like courts elsewhere, thought "a nation must have inherently the power to save itself," and that included the state legislature's determination that national self-preservation "depends upon a unity of effort on the part of all the citizens." The state must be ever watchful that "evil seeds" were not sown among the citizenry that might eventually bear the fruit of "disloyalty and disrespect."[16] Governmental fear of a nefarious Johnny Appleseed planting evil fruit across the nation did not subside with the end of open hostilities in Europe.

The internal security apparatus erected at both the federal and the state level at the beginning of the Cold War not only created a sweeping system of loyalty oaths but also an ever-present threat of ad hoc investigations. According to one report, "by 1956 no less than forty-two states, and more than two thousand county and municipal subdivisions and state and local administrative commissions required loyalty oaths" of people from lawyers to residents in public housing to professional wrestlers.[17] In 1948, former federal appellate judge Thurman Arnold wrote an essay on "How *Not* to Get Investigated" based in part on his own private practice in Washington, D.C. Among his tips, "Do not subscribe to the *New Republic* or the *Nation*, or any other liberal publication." Someone might get the wrong idea. Arnold thought such surveillance by government loyalty boards was not only "a poor way of fighting a cold war against Russia," but it could also "never strengthen a democracy." "In independence of thought and action is the safety of our country. It is not difficult to drive such independence out of government."[18]

Independence of thought was not always welcome in the public schools. The notorious Feinberg Law of 1949 directed New York's board of regents to adopt rules to identify and remove such teachers and create a list of prohibited subversive organizations.[19] As a state court said in upholding the law, "We are not so naive as to accept as gospel the argument that a teacher who believes in the destruction of our form of Government will not affect his students." The state had a particular interest in the thoughts of those who would be molding "the childish mind."[20] The government did not need to monitor the specific things that a teacher might say in the classroom. It was safer, and constitutionally adequate in the immediate postwar period, for the state to identify those who might say subversive things. The best way to stop teachers from sharing dangerous ideas with their students was to identify teachers who themselves held dangerous ideas and to remove them from the classroom.

The fate of young schoolchildren might have been of particular interest to legislators in the postwar period, but the intellectual environment of college students did not escape their attention. During and after the First World War, colleges were less likely than primary and secondary schools to be "directly controlled by statute," but less direct "pressure from public opinion or donors" worked to ensure at both private and public universities that only "'safe and sane' men are hired" and that "controversial matters" not be discussed on campus. The University of Pennsylvania explained when it fired a philosophy professor who had praised the Soviet Union, it is "incompatible for a man to take a stand on a public issue and at the same time to retain the critical state of mind necessary for research in philosophy and teaching." It went without saying that publishing a book on *The American College and its Rulers*, as one professor did in 1926, was a firing offense.[21]

Unsurprisingly, the demand that professors not take stands on public issues was not evenly applied. The appointment of famed British philosopher Bertrand Russell to a position at City College was overturned by a state court as appalling and unlawful in part because the taxpayers of New York "are not spending that money nor was that money appropriated for the purpose of employing teachers who are not of good moral character." In addition to being a notorious atheist, "Mr. Russell has taught in his books immoral and salacious doctrines" relating to premarital sex.[22] University officials routinely barred from campus such outside speakers as celebrated defense attorney Clarence Darrow and ACLU director Roger Baldwin. Dangerous ideas of many sorts were to be kept out of the universities, and faculty advisors of student groups extending such invitations could find themselves out of a job.

The Cold War and the Universities

After the Second World War, politicians began more directly to intervene on college campuses. At a confirmation hearing for new regents of the University of Washington in 1947, a state senator voiced the emerging worry:

> There isn't a student who has attended this University who has not been taught subversive activities and when they come home it is very hard for parents to change their minds. I have reports that show definitely that five professors teach subversive activities at the school and other reports that the number is as high as thirty.[23]

Seeing the shifting political winds, the newly installed president of the university cautioned the faculty that they had "a special obligation to deal in a scholarly way with controversial questions," and that they should refrain from giving voice to "half-formed judgments and prejudices."[24] Under pressure from the state legislature, the board of regents of the University of California tried to take matters into its own hands in 1949. It amended an existing oath requiring that university employees swear their loyalty to the federal and state constitutions by adding a further requirement that they foreswear membership in any organization that was subversive of the American government. The board's decision sparked an unusually large and broad coalition of faculty to oppose the new oath. A letter to the university president from the newly formed Group for Academic Freedom asserted that "the one thing that has kept freedom in American universities is the traditional right of teachers to be judged by their peers as to ability and integrity." Once the principle was accepted that the regents could impose their own conditions on the professors to be employed by the university, how could students have faith that the faculty hired under such conditions would "still be free to speak and teach

and write the unadulterated truth."[25] Professors should be
judged by their overt acts demonstrating misconduct, not by
their beliefs and associations. The regents were unmoved and
voted to dismiss any faculty members who refused to sign the
new loyalty oath.[26]

University professors were widely required to attest that
they had not belonged to subversive organizations like the
Communist Party. Texas went so far as to require that authors
of school textbooks attest that they had not been a member of
a movement that had been "designated as totalitarian, fascist,
communist, or subversive" or that advocated "acts of force
or violence to deny others their rights" or sought to "alter
the form of Government of the United States by unconstitu-
tional means."[27] Refusing to testify in an un-American affairs
investigation was specified to be grounds for dismissal from a
faculty position. State university officials, like the president of
the Ohio State University, declared that refusal to cooperate
with anti-Communism investigations was "gross insubordina-
tion" and "conduct clearly inimical to the best interests of the
university," which created "serious doubt as to [a professor's]
fitness for the position" and justified the stripping of tenure and
termination of employment.[28] A New York court concluded
that "the assertion of the privilege against self-incrimination is
equivalent to a resignation" from a teaching post.[29] States like
Arkansas required professors to divulge the organizations with
which they had been associated. States from Washington to
North Carolina banned from college campuses speakers who
had advocated the overthrow of the American government.[30]

The fear of tenured radicals was not limited to state universities by any means. When Dwight Eisenhower left Columbia
University after a brief stint as its president to move to the
White House, he delivered a farewell address to a crowd of
faculty and students. He confessed that before arriving at
Columbia he "heard of this constant rumor and black suspicion that our universities were cut and honeycombed with

subversion." He agreed to accept that job only if the university would rid itself of anyone adhering to "any kind of traitorous doctrine." In "a war of great ideologies," "no man flying a war plane . . . can possibly be more important than the teacher." Fortunately, in his short stay he had not found a Communist "behind every brick on the campus," but he expected the campus to remain vigilant after he had left.[31]

As pressure built on universities to dispel this "black suspicion," Yale University president Charles Seymour declared, "There will be no witch-hunt at Yale because there will be no witches. We do not intend to hire Communists."[32] The Association of American Universities tried to walk a fine line in a 1953 statement. On the one hand, it insisted against outside critics that "the scholar's mission requires the study and examination of unpopular ideas, of ideas considered abhorrent and even dangerous." The scholar "has no obligation to be silent in the face of popular disapproval," and the teacher had the responsibility and right "to express his own critical opinion and the reasons for holding it," limited only by "the requirements of citizenship, of professional competence, and good taste." At the same time, those appointed to a university faculty had "the affirmative obligation of being diligent and loyal in citizenship" and a particular obligation to reject the Communist Party principles of "the fomenting of world-wide revolution as a step to seizing power; the use of falsehood and deceit as normal means of persuasion; thought control – the dictation of doctrines which must be accepted and taught by all party members."[33]

Beyond the general dangers of potentially exposing students to radical ideas, membership in the Communist Party posed a particular challenge for the scholarly profession. The president of Cornell University initially told his board of trustees that a professor who was exposed as a Communist should not be fired unless there was evidence of specific misconduct, but he later changed his stance given that "it is part of the established technique of Communistic activity to resort to deceit and treachery." A dean at the University of Michigan echoed this view, suggesting to the regents there that "the fundamental doctrines of the Communist Party deny to its members that freedom to think and speak independently which is the basis of University policy."[34] If the point of academic freedom was to secure the independence necessary for scholars and teachers to express the truth as they best understand it, membership in the Community Party was inherently incompatible with that ideal. They had compromised themselves as scholars in exactly the way that the Group for Academic Freedom feared that professors at the University of California would be compromised if the regents there could impose ideological purity tests on the faculty. A member of the Communist Party is not, in the words of the president of the University of Washington, "a free man." So long as they were faithful to the party, they could not be "a free seeker after the truth." It is not just that the professor with radical views professes ideas that some find dangerous; it is that the professor pledged to the Communist Party "is chained to a party dogma."[35]

The social democratic philosopher Sidney Hook was perhaps most vocal in highlighting this concern. The problem was not, he argued, one of national security. "At no time was the number of Communists in colleges sufficiently high to warrant the slightest concern that they would undermine our national security." The problem was rather one of "professional ethics and professional integrity." "If a teacher honestly reaches the conclusion that the Communist or fascist position on any subject is valid, that is one thing," Hook thought, "but if the teacher is pledged in advance to indoctrinate, as members of Communist and fascist parties are, that is something quite different."[36] Such considerations led even the philosopher Arthur O. Lovejoy, one of the key players in founding the American Association of University Professors, to conclude that membership in the Communist Party was incompatible with the core societal justification for granting freedom to academics, which was that those academics would then provide "his honest report of what *he* finds, or believes, to be true, after careful study of the problems with which he deals."[37]

Why bother targeting hard-to-monitor classroom speech when it was possible to use a broader brush and remove instructors for their outside political expression and activity? At least initially state governments understood themselves to have a free hand to purge subversives from the ranks of the faculty and did not need to worry over what those subversives were actually doing in the classroom. In 1952, for example, the U.S. Supreme Court upheld New York's Feinberg Law in *Adler v. Board of Education of the City of New York*. Justice Sherman Minton wrote for the Court that "the state has a vital concern" with those employed in its educational institutions and has the right to "maintain the integrity of the schools as part of ordered society." The state has the power "to protect the schools from pollution and thereby to defend its own existence," and individuals have a right to choose between their freedom to advocate radical doctrines and the privilege of government employment.[38] Minton's view would soon fall out of favor, as the Court confronted the application of anti-subversive policies in higher education, and as the Court became more civil libertarian.

4

The First Amendment
Comes to Campus

The Cold War tested the strength of the commitment of American higher education to academic freedom principles. By the postwar period American universities had largely adopted the position that tenure-line faculty could not be treated as at-will employees and dismissed whenever they became politically inconvenient, as they had been at the beginning of the twentieth century. Professors were widely understood, by university officials at least, to enjoy some degree of academic freedom, and those principles were backstopped by a system of tenure protections that meant that professors could not be fired without a demonstration of good cause.

Those academic freedom principles were not simply rolled back in the context of the Cold War, but there was substantial pressure to find a way of accommodating them to the needs of the anti-subversive drive. Under myriad circumstances, expressing subversive ideas could be characterized as a sufficient cause to merit removal. In many cases, the emerging system of contracts and customs was overridden by statute and administrative activism.

At least in the context of state universities, the Court began to bolster contracts and customs with the First Amendment.

Even if universities changed their policies or legislatures over-rode those university policies, the Court began to insist that there were some constitutional limitations on how state universities treated state university professors.

At the outset of what became known as the Second Red Scare, it was not at all obvious that the First Amendment imposed much of a limit on how state legislatures could regulate what was taught in state university classrooms. When all was said and done and the McCarthy era faded into the past, it was still not terribly clear how much of an obstacle the First Amendment posed to politicians who wanted to meddle in the operations of state universities. The Court had declared that academic freedom had constitutional weight under the First Amendment, but it had not provided much guidance for what that should mean in practice. Even so, merely recognizing that academic freedom should be factored into constitutional analysis marked a sea change in the law.

The "Hired Man"

In 1915, the board of trustees at the University of Pennsylvania declined to renew the appointment of one of the professors at the Wharton School of Business. The board declined to give an explanation for its actions, but everyone assumed that they knew what had happened. Scott Nearing was a brash young professor, a Penn alumnus, and one of the most popular teachers at the university. He was also a vocal socialist. He did not plan to go quietly, and his termination soon became a *cause célèbre*, sparking an extended debate in the nation's newspapers about the freedom of university professors to teach what they believed.

Perhaps it should not have been surprising for a man "with an unholy genius for getting his name in the papers" that the *New York Times* deemed it front-page news that Nearing had been "ousted," and the University of Pennsylvania was put under a microscope. The *Washington Post* assured its readers that the ouster was for "the radical views which Prof. Nearing has been airing upon the lecture platform for some time," while the *Cincinnati Enquirer* instead thought he had been dismissed "because of his persistent advocacy of free speech." The president of the New York chapter of the Penn alumni association explained, "I am in favor of freedom of speech, but not license." He opposed the "radical minority," who thought that professors could say whatever they liked "on all questions, regardless of what the university stands for." Penn could not tolerate instructors who "stand up in classrooms and preach agnostics to boys who have come to college from Christian homes," or mounted "academic attacks on any class of persons such as men who have acquired great wealth." The University had no obligation "to stand sponsor for Nearing's views."[1] Meanwhile, the son-in-law of the business school's namesake organized a petition campaign, urging the governor to withhold the state's substantial annual appropriation to the school, and students and faculty rallied to Nearing's defense.

The Nearing case crystallized the emerging disagreement over whether a university professor was, as the philosopher John Dewey phrased it, "a hired man." A more senior and conservative professor at the business school warned the trustees that they were giving truth to the suspicion "that professors at the University of Pennsylvania are virtually employees of a few representatives of inherited or acquired wealth." Were professors simply to be "the mouthpieces of rich men," to be relieved of their duties whenever they stepped out of line? If so, then their scholarly judgments would be treated as little more than bought-and-paid-for propaganda.[2]

Many university leaders of the time believed just that. The chancellor of Syracuse University weighed in on the Nearing controversy by asking whether a newspaper would continue to employ an editorial writer "if he were to disregard the things for which the paper stands." When a professor is hired by a university, an editorial in the Penn alumni magazine explained, "he becomes in a sense her spokesman," and as such he "thereby relinquishes his right to complete freedom of speech." Even the lonely Penn trustee sympathetic to Nearing's case thought that members of the faculty had the right to express their opinions only "in a proper manner, upon proper occasions, and with proper respect for the dignity of their relationship to the university" and, "when an individual teacher's methods, language, and temperament provoke continued and widespread criticism alike from parents of students and from the general public," the trustees had an obligation to remove that individual from the faculty.[3]

The "hired man" perspective reflected both a sensibility and a legal relationship. Many university leaders in the early twentieth century believed that professors were in fact paid to parrot the beliefs of powerful stakeholders and that ruffling too many feathers by expressing unorthodox opinions was sufficient cause for terminating a maverick member of the faculty. The law surrounding university employment backed university leaders who wanted to take that approach to their faculty. That was as true at public universities as it was at private universities. The trustees at the University of Pennsylvania were within their rights to fire Scott Nearing for his radical views, and the regents at Pennsylvania State University could have done the same. As one education law expert noted in the 1930s, "professorial tenure is made insecure in many state institutions by statutes of the state or ordinances of the governing board making professors removable at the pleasure of the board, or whenever the board determines that the interests of the institution require it."[4] As another author explained, "higher education, like other administrative activities of government, is completely under the regulating power of the law-making body," and the legislature was free to say that the board of regents "can remove employees at will."[5]

The Wisconsin state supreme court encapsulated the state of the law when informing a professor who had been summarily dismissed by a state school that, "he had unfortunately become embroiled in controversies which impaired his usefulness as a teacher, and threatened the success, peace, and harmony of the school." There had been "a contention between the president and the professors and students," and the professor had become "involved" in that dispute. The discretionary power of the regents to fire a professor who had made himself disagreeable was "unquestionable."[6] Those who held their office at the pleasure of the board of regents had no legal recourse if their termination had "been due to prejudice or passion."[7] The prospect that constitutional limitations might hinder the authority of regents to fire controversial professors was so remote as to be not worth mentioning prior to the Second World War.

Nonetheless, as states ratcheted up their efforts to ferret out professors with subversive ideas, some saw glimmers of hope that courts might intervene. Among the hopeful was a young Ted Sorensen, soon to become the right-hand man of Senator John F. Kennedy. He pointed out that the Supreme Court had set out a "general limitation applicable to all state action," that "there should be no suppression in the marketplace of thought and free discussion." No matter how deferential the Court had become after the New Deal, it had still "given a 'preferred position' to the rights of the First Amendment." Most importantly, the Court had just declared that those robust First Amendment protections applied "in public schools 'owned' by the state."[8] In the midst of the Second World War, the Court had made waves in holding that public schoolchildren could not be compelled to say the Pledge of Allegiance. In *West Virginia Board of Education v. Barnette*, the Court proclaimed, "If there is any fixed star in our constitutional constellation, it is that no official, high or petty, can prescribe what shall be orthodox in politics, nationalism, religion, or other matters of opinion."[9]

A lower court in New York had come to the same conclu-sion about where the law was headed. Asked to assess the constitutionality of the state's Feinberg Law, directing the board of regents to exclude from public employment teachers who belonged to subversive organizations, the judge thought the Flag Salute Case had demonstrated that "legislation which penalizes the free expression of views or espousal of doctrines must receive . . . the closest judicial scrutiny." In the court's view, the legislative effort to keep radicals out of the schools did not survive that close scrutiny. "The court finds it hard to believe that it is necessary to resort to witch-hunting in our schools to displace misfits."[10]

Other commentators – and other judges – were not convinced that anything had changed when it came to First Amendment limitations on public employment. "Courts are," one concluded in predicting the likely fate of the Feinberg Law, "disinclined to see the substantive liberties of the First Amendment . . . directly involved in cases such as this where the problem may be seen as essentially one of disqualification from the privilege of teaching." While *Barnette* might have been momentous for student speech rights, it might have been much less consequential for the speech rights of their instruc-tors. No one had a right to public employment, and thus "the right conditioned by the Feinberg Law does not appear to be within the protection of the First Amendment."[11]

It was not the Flag Salute Case but an entirely different and even more recent decision of the Supreme Court that seemed to cast doubt on any judicial recognition of academic freedom. In *United Public Workers v. Mitchell*, the justices had upheld against constitutional challenge the authority of Congress to pass the Hatch Act, which prohibited a large swath of govern-ment employees from engaging in many political activities. "For regulation of employees," the Court held, "it is not nec-essary that the act regulated be anything more than an act reasonably deemed by Congress to interfere with the efficiency of the public service." It was enough that Congress had deter-mined that public employees engaging in certain kinds of political activities "is bad." Courts should not scrutinize those legislative decisions too closely.[12]

Judges across the country understood the message that state university professors were still hired men, who could be let go if their political views were not welcome. The supreme court in New Jersey thought loyalty oaths for state university professors was "no effort to control thought," because individuals asked to take such an oath faced "no personal penalty for noncon-formity."[13] Being excluded from government jobs was not an injury that the Constitution recognized. As the supreme court of Oklahoma pointed out, "the required loyalty oath do[es] not deprive public officials and employees of property or liberty without due process of law. . . . The act does not purport to take away their right to teach. Public institutions do not have to hire or retain employees except on terms suitable to them."[14] The high court in New York thought the same in reversing the decision of the lower court on the constitutional valid-ity of the Feinberg Law. "A public employee has no vested, proprietary right to his position which transcends the public interest or the general welfare of the community he serves." The state legislature had a perfect right to adopt measures that it believed necessary to prevent government employees from using "their office or position to advocate and teach subversive doctrines."[15] As the famed progressive judge Benjamin Cardozo had said decades earlier, the legislature had a free hand to impose restrictions on government employees, so long as those policies bear "some relation to the advancement of the public welfare" – and the "legislature has unquestionably the widest latitude of judgment in determining whether such a relation exists."[16] The rights of government employees as individuals gave way to the public interest as it was deemed necessary by the democratically elected government. Professors might contract for academic freedom, but there could not be a meaningful constitutional protection for academic freedom. Or so well-trained lawyers thought in the Eisenhower era.

"The Theory of Our Constitution"

The Court was in no position to extend First Amendment protection to radical speech on campus, however, if the First Amendment did not protect radical speech anywhere else. At the time that the AAUP was organizing, it was far from established that radical political speech as such enjoyed any constitutional protection. American courts had long recognized the substantial discretion of government officials in punishing speech or writing that was thought to be potentially dangerous to the community. Even radical professors were not of first concern to state governments worried that incendiary speech might light a fuse that could result in literal bombings, but the general understanding of freedom of speech in the United States in the early twentieth century did not place much value on speech outside the social or political mainstream.

When the United States entered the First World War, Congress moved swiftly to criminalize speech or writing that hampered the war effort, or at least that might be thought by the government to hamper the war effort. The dim view of "disloyal" speech by government officials was shared by many in academia. Columbia University president Nicholas Murray Butler warned his campus against "vice and cowardice." While American entry into the war was still uncertain, "we gave complete freedom, as is our wont and as becomes a university, freedom of assembly, freedom of speech, and freedom of publication to all members of the University." But "conditions sharply changed" when Congress declared war.

What had been tolerated before became intolerable now. What had been wrongheadedness was now sedition. What had been folly was now treason. . . . there is and will be no place in Columbia University, either on the rolls of its faculties or on the rolls of its students, for any person who opposes or who counsels opposition to the effective enforcement of the laws of the United States, or who acts, speaks or writes treason.[17]

When Butler put words into action and fired a professor, he received national attention. The *Pittsburgh Gazette-Times* was not atypical in editorializing that "In ordinary times the teaching staff of a university may well be jealous of its prerogatives of deciding what shall be taught and how. When the country is on the verge of war the trustees would seem to have a duty to make sure that the doctrines presented in classes cannot be construed as disloyal."[18] The progressive economist Richard K. Ely did not disagree. "We cannot take the same position in time of war as we take in time of peace. . . . A man who gives utterance to opinions which hinder us in this awful struggle deserves to be fired."[19] Professorial speech that verged on the unlawful could find no shelter in the universities.

The first half of the twentieth century saw a general flowering of First Amendment doctrine. The justices both reflected and helped shape a new constitutional culture that placed greater value on protecting rather than suppressing ideas that might unsettle the status quo. That shift in the constitutional culture was a necessary precondition for the extension of academic freedom to such dangerous ideas.[20]

By the time of the Cold War, the Court had already made it clear that radical political ideas were not in and of themselves beyond the protection of the First Amendment. In doing so, it had also reframed the ethos of the First Amendment itself. Justice Oliver Wendell Holmes did more than try to expand the margins of free-speech protections when he argued that:

[T]he best test of truth is the power of the thought to get itself accepted in the competition of the market, and that truth is the only ground upon which their wishes safely can be carried out. That, at any rate, is the theory of our Constitution. It is an experiment, as all life is an experiment. Every year, if not every day, we have to wager our salvation upon some prophecy based upon imperfect knowledge. While that experiment is part of our system, I think that we should be eternally vigilant against attempts to check the expression of opinions that we loathe and believe to be fraught with death, unless they so imminently threaten immediate interference with the lawful and pressing purposes of the law that an immediate check is required to save the country.

Holmes posited a new "theory of our Constitution" that was grounded in making space for "opinions that we loathe" and countering ideas only with argument and persuasion.[21] Writing just four years after the AAUP had issued its Declaration of Principles, Holmes was elevating the marketplace of ideas to a central place in the American constitutional order. Tolerating, rather than suppressing, radical ideas was at the heart of the American democratic experiment. If that was true at the street corner, it was surely true in the lecture hall as well.

Again and again, Holmes hammered at this theme. "If, in the long run, the beliefs expressed in proletarian dictatorship are destined to be accepted by the dominant forces of the community, the only meaning of free speech is that they should be given their chance and have their way."[22] Or "if there is any principle of the Constitution that more imperatively calls for attachment than any other, it is the principle of free thought – not free thought for those who agree with us, but freedom for the thought that we hate." For this new vision of the Constitution, "it cannot show lack of attachment to the principles of the Constitution that she thinks that it can be improved."[23] Justice Louis Brandeis added, "Those who won our independence believed that the final end of the State was to make men free to develop their faculties, and that, in its government, the deliberative forces should prevail over the arbitrary."[24] Such views initially expressed in dissent over time found their way into the Court's majority.[25]

In truth, Holmes, unlike Brandeis, was a reluctant convert to the cause of free speech. He had long been skeptical of the idea of individual rights and preferred to think instead in terms of social interests. Even near the end of his life, he confessed, "I think the argument for free speech, devoutly as I believe in it, is not entirely easy." When pursuing its goals, the state does not "hesitate very much over even conscientious scruples," and Holmes did not think it should.[26] His own harrowing experience as a young Union soldier in the Civil War seems to have helped convince him that "when men differ in taste as to the kind of world they want, the only thing left to do is to go to work killing."[27] Free speech and democratic elections helped lay bare the dominant power in the community at least and hopefully reduced the need for violence. But, as Holmes was writing his opinions on the importance of the "freedom for the thought that we hate," he was immersed in tales of a war being waged at Harvard University. Boston conservatives were pressuring Harvard to push out of the faculty some of the justice's own progressive friends, including a young Felix Frankfurter. Even as he was attempting to steer First Amendment jurisprudence in a new direction, he was urging greater tolerance for "dangerous men" at his old stomping grounds in Cambridge.[28]

The vision of the Constitution advanced by Holmes and Brandeis still put some speech outside the bounds of constitutional protection, but it not only brought far more speech under the umbrella of the First Amendment it also placed the contestation over ideas at the heart of the American constitutional project. The state could rule out violent action, but it could not rule out the possibility of radical political change. If the First Amendment enshrined the belief that the ideas we hate have to be overcome through argument rather than coercion, then it was a repudiation of the American constitutional experiment for the state to attempt to suppress disfavored ideas. The very "theory of our Constitution" is that ideas we think are true must be put through the crucible of criticism and that ideas we hate must be allowed to have their say. As Justice Frank Murphy emphasized in a different First Amendment setting in the 1940s: "It is our proud achievement to have demonstrated that unity and strength are best accomplished not by enforced orthodoxy of views, but by diversity of opinion through the fullest possible measure of freedom of conscience and thought."[29] Justice Robert Jackson kicked an important leg out from under the state's authority to stifle dissent in schools in the Flag Salute Case during the Second World War, declaring, "If there is any fixed star in our constitutional constellation, it is that no official, high or petty, can prescribe what shall be orthodox in politics, nationalism, religion, or other matters of opinion, or force citizens to confess by word or act their faith therein." The very "purpose of the First Amendment" is to protect "from all official control" "the sphere of intellect and spirit."[30]

By the start of the Cold War, the "principle of free thought" had been enshrined as among the highest of constitutional ideals. The tolerance of free speech did not just set outer bounds on the imperative of maintaining public order. Protecting free speech was the constitutional imperative itself. The implications for American state universities could not be easily ignored.

Limiting the "Flow of Ideas into the Minds of Men"

If freedom of thought is a core constitutional value, then impinging on academic freedom could readily be seen as a betrayal of the constitutional enterprise. Across the 1950s and into the 1960s, the Court began to give constitutional recognition to principles of academic freedom. When Justice Minton wrote for the Court, upholding New York's Feinberg Law in

1952, former Yale Law professor Justice William O. Douglas wrote a dissent, giving academic freedom a toehold in the First Amendment. He began necessarily with the problem of government employee speech. Minton relied on the traditional assumption famously captured in an early Holmesian quip: "The petitioner may have a constitutional right to talk politics, but he has no constitutional right to be a policeman."[31] The majority of the justices reaffirmed that everyone had "the right under our law to assemble, speak, think and believe as they will," but the privilege of working for the state could be withheld from those who expressed radical ideas. If individuals "do not choose to work on such terms, they are at liberty to retain their beliefs and associations and go elsewhere."[32]

Douglas, joined by Justice Hugo Black, by contrast, could not "find in our constitutional scheme the power of a state to place its employees in the category of denying them freedom of thought and expression."[33] Douglas quickly turned his attention to the implications of anti-subversive measures operating in schools and emphasized how they would necessarily encroach on the intellectual freedom that schools should be fostering. The intrinsic problem of "guilt by association" raised by the requirement of identifying current and past membership in potentially subversive groups "is certain to raise havoc with academic freedom." Teachers would fear becoming enmeshed in such investigations "when the witch hunt is on." As a result, those subjected to such requirements "will tend to shrink from any association that stirs controversy" and "freedom of expression will be stifled." More directly, "the law inevitably turns the school system into a spying project." With students and parents becoming "informers," "it is a system which searches for hidden meanings in a teacher's utterances." Where "teachers are under constant surveillance," "there can be no academic freedom." Where every utterance could become grounds for political reprisal, "supineness and dogmatism take the place of inquiry." Such laws force teachers into mouthing "the orthodox view," "the conventional thought" and, to avoid any "adventurous thinking." "A deadening dogma takes the place of free inquiry."[34] Justice Hugo Black wrote separately, without using the term "academic freedom," but to similarly emphasize that "these laws rest on the belief that government should supervise and limit the flow of ideas into the minds of men." The First Amendment was designed to prevent "a transient majority" from being able "to select the idea people can think about."[35]

Douglas and Black were both New Dealers to the core, and they had no doubt that the conservative Court of years past had gone too far in obstructing the will of democratic majorities when it came to regulating businesses and the operation of the economy, but they thought the democratic regulation of speech was different. Douglas, the son of a west coast preacher, and Black, a former senator from Alabama, were distinguishing themselves on the postwar Court as near free-speech absolutists. Delivering the James Madison Lecture at New York University Law School in 1963, Douglas observed that "a regimented society must control speech if people are to be subdued." By contrast, "discourse and debate" in America "were to be unlimited."[36] Black had delivered the same lecture just a few years earlier and had been similarly emphatic.

Since the earliest days philosophers have dreamed of a country where the mind and spirit of man would be free; where there would be no limits to inquiry; where men would be free to explore the unknown and to challenge the most deeply rooted beliefs and principles. Our First Amendment was a bold effort to adopt this principle – to establish a country with no legal restrictions of any kind upon the subjects people could investigate, discuss, and deny. The Framers knew, better perhaps than we do today, the risks they were taking. They knew that free speech might be the friend of change and revolution. But they also knew that it was always the deadliest enemy of tyranny. With this knowledge they still believed that the ultimate happiness and security of a nation lies in its ability to explore, to change, to grow and ceaselessly adapt itself to new knowledge born of inquiry free from any kind of governmental control over the mind and spirit of man. Loyalty comes from love of good government, not fear of a bad one.[37]

Douglas and Black might have taken the lead in advancing a civil libertarian position on freedom of speech in the postwar Court, but they were not alone in concluding that tolerance for dissenting views was an important distinguishing feature between a liberal democracy and a totalitarian dictatorship.

The Court's majority reached a different conclusion from the one it had in *Adler*, when confronted with an Oklahoma statute that the justices thought swept more broadly than the Feinberg Law. Dismissing government employees who had no specific knowledge of the subversive purposes of the organizations that they had joined "offends due process."[38] This time, former Harvard law professor Justice Felix Frankfurter wrote separately for himself and Douglas in laying out specific concerns with how such laws affected teachers.[39] The case from Oklahoma involved not secondary-school teachers but members of the faculty and staff at the Oklahoma Agricultural and Mechanical College (now Oklahoma State University). Frankfurter did not use the specific term "academic freedom," but he thought "in view of the nature of the teacher's relation to the effective exercise of the rights which are safeguarded by the Bill of Rights and the Fourteenth Amendment, inhibition of freedom of thought, and of action upon thought, in the case of teachers, brings the safeguards of those amendments vividly into operation." Teachers were, Frankfurter warned, "the priests of democracy," who "must be exemplars of open-mindedness and free inquiry." They "must be free to sift evanescent doctrine, qualified by time and circumstance, from that restless, enduring process of extending the bounds of understanding and wisdom." He concluded with an extended quote from Robert Hutchins, the former dean of Yale Law School and influential president of the University of Chicago, that began:

> [A] university is a place that is established and will function for the benefit of society, provided it is a center of independent thought. It is a center of independent thought and criticism that is created in the interest of the progress of society, and the one reason that we know that every totalitarian government must fail is that no totalitarian government is prepared to face the consequences of creating free universities.[40]

The quote was drawn from testimony that Hutchins had recently given before a House committee investigating tax-exempt foundations, where he was grilled in part about allegations of subversive activities at the University of Chicago. Hutchins there contended that the Communists were best met by Americans maintaining and developing "the basic sources of our strength," namely "the Western tradition of freedom, freedom of thought, freedom of discussion, and freedom of association." As a university president, Hutchins thought he had an obligation to take "immediate action" if any member of the faculty "had been engaged in subversive activity," but mere membership in questionable organizations or interest in "the study of Marxism" did not disqualify someone from being a member in good standing of the scholarly community.[41]

The Court soon had another opportunity to consider the impact of anti-subversive measures on the academic activities of universities. The attorney general of New Hampshire launched an investigation of Paul Sweezy, a Marxist economist who had left a lecturer position at Harvard University to found the socialist journal *Monthly Review*. In 1954, Sweezy gave a guest lecture in an undergraduate class at the University of New Hampshire. Sweezy refused to answer questions about the lecture, as he had refused to answer questions about his other activities, and was held in contempt. Writing for the Court, Chief Justice Earl Warren observed: "We believe that there unquestionably was an invasion of petitioner's liberties in the areas of academic freedom and free expression – areas in which the government should be extremely reticent to tread." He then elaborated:

> The essentiality of freedom in the community of American universities is almost self-evident. No one should underestimate the vital role in a democracy that is played by those who guide and train our youth. To impose any strait jacket upon the intellectual leaders in our colleges and universities would imperil the future of our Nation. No field of education is so thoroughly comprehended by man that new discoveries cannot yet be made. Particularly is that true in the social sciences, where few, if any, principles are accepted as absolutes. Scholarship cannot flourish in an atmosphere of suspicion and distrust. Teachers and students must always remain free to inquire, to study and to evaluate, to gain new maturity and understanding; otherwise, our civilization will stagnate and die.

The state supreme court had admitted as much but thought the state's interest justified the imposition on Sweezy's liberty. The Warren Court disagreed: "We do not now conceive of any circumstance wherein a state interest would justify infringement of rights in these fields." But the Court ultimately chose instead to reverse the state courts on the inadequacy of the legislature's authorization of such an intrusive investigation.[42] Frankfurter, joined by Justice John Marshall Harlan, thought the majority's alternative grounds were in fact more intrusive to state authority.

Frankfurter preferred instead to rest the case solely on the academic freedom question. The state's justification was inadequate to overcome the "grave harm resulting from governmental intrusion into the intellectual life of a university."

The intellectual life of a university "must be left as unfettered as possible" and could be justified only "for reasons that are exigent and obviously compelling." Frankfurter thought obvious

> the dependence of a free society on free universities. This means the exclusion of governmental intervention in the intellectual life of a university. It matters little whether such intervention occurs avowedly or through action that inevitably tends to check the ardor and fearlessness of scholars, qualities at once so fragile and so indispensable for fruitful academic labor.

Frankfurter again concluded with a lengthy quote, in this case from a statement on open universities in South Africa, ending with, "It is the business of a university to provide that atmosphere which is most conducive to speculation, experiment and creation. It is an atmosphere in which there prevail 'the four essential freedoms' of a university – to determine for itself on academic grounds who may teach, what may be taught, how it shall be taught, and who may be admitted to study."[43]

In *Shelton v. Tucker*, the Court struck down an Arkansas statute that required teachers at public educational institutions, including universities, to file an annual affidavit listing all of their organizational affiliations. When the Arkansas legislature adopted Act 10 in 1958, the NAACP was as much a concern as the Communist Party.[44] The Court recognized, as it had in *Adler*, that the state had the right "to investigate the competence and fitness of those whom it hires to teach in its schools," but also noted, as it had in *Sweezy*, that "[t]he vigilant protection of constitutional freedoms is nowhere more vital than in the community of American schools." Ultimately, the majority thought the state's inquiry was too sweeping and indiscriminate.[45]

Notably, Frankfurter now found himself in dissent. Although heedful of the danger of "crude intrusions by the state into the atmosphere of creative freedom in which alone the spirit and

mind of a teacher can fruitfully function," he thought that academic freedom "in its most creative reaches, is dependent in
no small part upon the careful and discriminating selection of
teachers." He did not think the record had yet established that
the state was using Act 10 "to further a scheme of terminating
the employment of teachers solely because of their membership in unpopular organizations."[46] As long as the state was
just asking questions, Frankfurter was not prepared to intervene.[47] A year after the Court struck down Arkansas's Act 10
in *Shelton*, the distinguished historian of the South C. Vann
Woodward reported that "academic freedom is still taking a
beating in the lower South."[48] The combination of Jim Crow
and the Cold War was proving especially damaging to free
inquiry in the states of the Old Confederacy, and the federal
courts were increasingly called upon to respond to legislative
impositions on academic freedom.

"A Special Concern of the First Amendment"

Near the end of the Warren Court, the justices had an opportunity to revisit the Feinberg Law and, in doing so, consolidate
the developments in the Court's thinking since *Adler* had been
decided fifteen years before. In *Keyishian v. Board of Regents*,
members of the faculty in the State University of New York
system had refused to sign certificates saying that they had
never been Communists. New Jersey state supreme court justice William Brennan had been picked by President Eisenhower
to succeed Justice Sherman Minton. Brennan quickly emerged
as one of the Court's most ardent defenders of free speech, and
he often had the votes on the Court to write his views into law.

Writing for the Court in 1967, Justice William Brennan
observed that "pertinent constitutional doctrines have since
rejected the premises upon which that conclusion [in *Adler*]
rested." The Court now thought the law was fatally vague and

overbroad. "The crucial consideration is that no teacher can know just where the line is drawn between 'seditious' and non-seditious utterances and acts." "Does the teacher who informs his class about the precepts of Marxism or the Declaration of Independence violate this prohibition?" "[D]oes the prohibition of distribution of matter 'containing' the doctrine [of the forceful overthrow of the existing government] bar histories of the evolution of Marxist doctrine or tracing the background of the French, American, or Russian revolutions?"[49]

The inevitable effect of the law was to interfere with constitutionally protected academic freedom.

> It would be a bold teacher who would not stay as far as possible from utterances or acts which might jeopardize his living by enmeshing him in this intricate machinery. The uncertainty as to the utterances and acts proscribed increases that caution in "those who believe the written law means what it says." *Baggett v. Bullitt*, 377 U.S. 360, 374 (1964). The result must be to stifle "that free play of the spirit which all teachers ought especially to cultivate and practice . . ." That probability is enhanced by the provisions requiring an annual review of every teacher to determine whether any utterance or act of his, inside the classroom or out, came within the sanctions of the laws.

Citing the cases since *Adler*, Brennan gave firm recognition of a constitutionalized academic freedom.

> Our Nation is deeply committed to safeguarding academic freedom, which is of transcendent value to all of us, and not merely to the teachers concerned. That freedom is therefore a special concern of the First Amendment, which does not tolerate laws that cast a pall of orthodoxy over the classroom.

Laws that trench on that freedom must be drawn with a "narrow specificity" that the anti-subversive laws lacked. "The danger of that chilling effect upon the exercise of vital First Amendment rights must be guarded against by sensitive tools which clearly inform teachers what is being proscribed."[50]

After *Keyishian*, a First Amendment interest in an individualized academic freedom seemed firmly established, if not entirely clear in its implications. Academic freedom was now recognized as "a special concern of the First Amendment," if not exactly a right comparable to classic First Amendment rules. The next term the Court struck down an anti-evolution statute with Justice Abe Fortas noting: "It is much too late to argue that the State may impose upon the teachers in its schools any conditions that it chooses, however restrictive they may be of constitutional guarantees."[51] The Cold War wave of anti-subversive measures by state legislatures had forced the Court to confront efforts to suppress professorial speech. In doing so, they recognized that universities are what law professor Paul Horwitz has called "First Amendment institutions" because of their central role in generating, investigating, and promulgating ideas.[52] Suppressing ideas in a university context poses a particular threat to the values that the First Amendment enshrines.

Unfortunately, after *Keyishian* in 1967, the Supreme Court has had little more to say about academic freedom. The Court has never retreated from Brennan's bold insistence that the Constitution "does not tolerate laws that cast a pall of orthodoxy over the classroom," but it has not provided much guidance about what that might mean in practice. Judges across the country have understood that academic freedom has a precious status under the First Amendment, but they have been left to their own devices in figuring out where those principles might lead and how they should be vindicated. The Supreme Court has largely sat on the sidelines in the battle over university classrooms, since the days in which the baby boomers were staging sit-ins at universities across the country. It seems unlikely that the Court can sit on the sidelines much longer. When it joins the fray, it will have to take on the important task of explaining how academic freedom fits together with all that the Court has said about the First Amendment since the 1960s, and how much weight academic freedom should have when placed in the balance against the interests of the state in controlling the delivery of higher education in public universities.

5

The Professor as a Government Employee

University professors may be the "priests of democracy" with which the First Amendment has a particular concern, but when they work at state universities they are still government employees. The Court has not clearly resolved the tension inherent in that framework. As government employees, professors can be disciplined or penalized for their conduct, including in some cases for their speech acts. Moreover, professors as employees are routinely evaluated in part on the content, or quality, of their professorial speech.

What then are the limits to when university officials acting as agents of the state can sanction members of the faculty for their speech, and what are the implications for legislative efforts to restrict university classroom teaching? In this chapter I offer an approach to reconciling constitutional protections for academic freedom with governmental supervision of its employees. In doing so I extend the principles that the Court has laid out regarding the First Amendment and government employee speech in the particular context of a university setting.

One might think that what the Court had said about academic freedom in response to the anti-subversive laws would

make the constitutionality of more recent legislative restrictions on university teaching an easy question. It did not. The
Court has said too little about how the First Amendment value
of academic freedom might limit government officials and has
sent too many mixed messages about how the government
might manage the speech of its employees. The Court now has
an opportunity to clarify how much constitutional protection
academic freedom might have, but an aggressive state legislature might currently assume that it has quite a bit of room
to maneuver in regulating faculty speech on state university
campuses.

It is worth emphasizing that it is possible to work with the
existing doctrinal tools to protect academic freedom. It might
be helpful if the Court were to go back to basics and make a
fresh start, but the justices need not be so bold. If the justices
are clear-headed, it should be possible to build on existing doctrine to provide adequate protection for academic freedom.
Equally importantly, lower court judges have already received
sufficient guidance from the Court about the constitutional
importance of academic freedom and need not defer to state
legislatures bent on restricting classroom speech. Academic
freedom advocates have understandably been disappointed by
how the Court has approached constitutional protections for
the speech of government employees in other settings, but
the Court has not yet repudiated its affirmation of the special
importance of academic freedom to the First Amendment and
that core commitment should shape our understanding of how
more recent doctrine should be interpreted and applied.

In order to sustain their new policy proposals, government
officials are urging courts to lean hard in the other direction.
They would have judges ignore what the Court said in *Keyishian*
in striking down the Feinberg Law in 1967 and give state governments unbridled discretion to suppress disfavored speech
in state universities. As the attorneys for the state of Florida
argued to a federal court, "The First Amendment does not

compel Florida to pay educators to advocate ideas, in its name, that it finds repugnant." State university professors "may not espouse in the classroom" ideas disfavored by the state, "while they are on the State clock, in exchange for a State paycheck."[1] Some lower court opinions make their position credible. When still serving as a circuit court judge, Justice Samuel Alito once wrote, "a public university professor does not have a First Amendment right to decide what will be taught in the class-room."[2] Other federal circuit courts have likewise concluded that academic freedom could not be understood to give "teach-ers the control of public school curricula."[3] Someone has to determine what ideas are to be taught in the classrooms of state universities. Should state legislatures have the final say?

Marvin Pickering and his Letter

The Court established a balancing test for assessing when governmental interests can override the First Amendment interests of a government employee in *Pickering v. Board of Education*.[4] Pointing to the academic freedom cases arising out of the McCarthy era, *Pickering* recognized that government employees had First Amendment rights that governments as employers had to respect, but also identified circumstances in which those rights could nonetheless be overridden. Decided just a year after *Keyishian*, *Pickering* continues to provide the basic doctrinal framework within which courts evaluate regulations on the speech of government employees, including state university professors.

Marvin Pickering was a public high-school science teacher on the outskirts of Chicago. In 1961, Pickering wrote a letter to the editor that was published in a local newspaper. The letter complained that the local school board "is trying to push tax-supported athletics down our throats." The school board and the school administration were stumping, without much success, for voter approval of a bond issue and tax increase, but Pickering contended that the school's existing financial resources were not being "properly managed." Pickering warned the voters that the school leadership practiced a "kind of totalitarianism" to prevent teachers from voicing such criticisms in public.

The school superintendent perhaps gave credence to Pickering's complaint that teachers were being threatened into silence. Pickering was promptly fired after his letter was published. The school board resolved that the teacher's letter contained "untrue and false statements" and improperly "impugned the motives, honesty, integrity, truthfulness, responsibility, and competence" of school officials. Pickering sued for reinstatement and damages. As his case made its way through the court system over the next several years, returning to his teaching job became increasingly irrelevant but the principle at issue remained of importance.

The Illinois state courts applied the traditional legal doctrines to uphold the board of education's actions. The issue was not, the state supreme court emphasized, "whether the board may be publicly subjected" to the type of accusations made in Pickering's letter, but rather "whether it must continue to employ one who publishes misleading statements which are reasonably believed to be detrimental to the schools." Whatever "freedom a private critic might have" to write such a letter, Pickering was no private critic. Moreover, the government was not threatening Pickering with civil suits or criminal prosecution. It had simply ended his government employment. "By choosing to teach in the public schools, plaintiff undertook the obligation to refrain from conduct, which in the absence of such a position he would have an undoubted right to engage in." A government employee "is no more entitled to harm the schools by speech than by incompetency, cruelty, negligence, immorality, or any other conduct for which there may be no legal sanction."[5]

In an 8–1 decision authored by Justice Thurgood Marshall, the U.S. Supreme Court firmly declared that this traditional understanding of the authority of government employers to sanction their employees for their speech was no longer good law. "To the extent that the Illinois Supreme Court's opinion may be read to suggest that teachers may constitutionally be compelled to relinquish the First Amendment rights they would otherwise enjoy as citizens to comment on matters of public interest in connection with the operation of the public schools in which they work, it proceeds on a premise that has been unequivocally rejected in numerous prior decisions of this Court." As Justice Marshall characterized the task going forward, "The problem in any case is to arrive at a balance between the interests of the teacher, as a citizen, in commenting upon matters of public concern and the interest of the State, as an employer, in promoting the efficiency of the public services it performs through its employees."[6] The First Amendment rights of government employees are not absolute, and they are necessarily more circumscribed than the speech of a private citizen. But government employees had a freedom of speech that their employers were constitutionally obliged to respect.

The *Pickering* Court identified both the circumstances in which employee speech is entitled to First Amendment protection and the conditions under which an employee can be disciplined for such speech. Government employee speech is entitled to First Amendment consideration when the employee "as a citizen" is "speaking upon matters of public concern." Even so, the government employer can punish an employee for such speech if, in this case, it could demonstrate that the teacher's speech "impeded the teacher's proper performance of his daily duties in the classroom" or "interfered with the regular operation of the schools generally." The government must have an interest in suppressing the employee's speech that is particular to the employment context and distinguishable from the government's general interest in suppressing such speech if it had come from an ordinary citizen.[7] Similarly and in a separate case, the Court concluded that a professor at a state university could not be dismissed specifically because he had provided testimony to a legislative committee that was critical of the board of regents. Even though the professor in that case did not possess tenure protections, the Court emphasized that a state university's decision not to renew a professor's contract "may not be predicated on his exercise of First and Fourteenth Amendment rights."[8] These landmark cases overturned decades of conventional wisdom about the authority of the government to punish its employees for speech it does not like, but they also dealt with the comparatively easy case of employees engaging in political debates in their private lives. School boards and boards of regents asserted that no line could be drawn between the private and professional lives of their employees, but the Court thought the government's interest in the personal activities of its employees was relatively limited.

That still left the more difficult question of speech that occurred on the job. It took more than a decade for the justices to take up that issue, but in *Connick v. Myers*, the Court further elaborated on the conditions in which government employee speech is protected. *Connick* arose in the context of a district attorney's office rather than a school, and it addressed internal speech within the office about office policies rather than speech in the political arena. Here the Court emphasized "the common-sense realization that government offices could not function if every employment decision became a constitutional matter." The employee's constitutional interest is at its highest when the government "sought to suppress the rights of public employees to participate in public affairs," as it had done in the anti-subversive cases or in *Pickering*. By contrast, "when employee expression cannot be fairly considered as relating to any matter of political, social, or other concern of the community," no substantial First Amendment interests arise that might hinder the government from sanctioning an employee for such speech. When an employee speaks "upon matters only of personal interest" or "internal office affairs," the courts should not intervene. The First Amendment does not "constitutionalize the employee grievance." The "content, form, and context of a given statement" helps determine whether it "addresses a matter of public concern." The *Connick* Court also elaborated on the government's interest in addressing "the disruption of the office and the destruction of working relationships" that might stem from an employee's speech but warned that "a stronger showing may be necessary if the employee's speech more substantially involved matters of public concern."[9]

The constitutional test laid out in *Pickering* and *Connick* continues to guide the courts today when confronting cases of government officials seeking to suppress the speech of government employees. As a threshold matter, courts are to ask whether the speech at issue involves a matter of public concern. Speech that is only of personal interest or is part of ordinary workplace activities enjoys no presumptive constitutional protection. Speech like Pickering's letter, however, addresses matters of broad public concern and is therefore entitled to some constitutional consideration. Cases that satisfy that threshold analysis must then be subjected to a balancing test. Employees are not automatically vindicated if the speech for which they are being disciplined falls within the scope of the First Amendment. The courts must weigh the employee's recognized right of free speech against the government's legitimate interest in maintaining a well-functioning workplace. Employee speech that disrupts the workplace and prevents a government agency from efficiently delivering its public services need not be tolerated. Pickering's letter might have been politically inconvenient for his superintendent and school board, but there was no evidence that the publication of his letter hampered Pickering's ability to do his job. The balance of considerations might come out differently in a different case.

The Trouble with *Garcetti*

Two decades after *Connick*, the Court returned to the issue of government employee speech, and the *Pickering* balancing test was significantly modified in *Garcetti v. Ceballos*. *Garcetti* dealt squarely with the fact that a good deal of the workplace communications of government employees involves matters of public concern, and thus could not be simply set aside as workplace grievances of no interest to the First Amendment. When talking about the public's business, government employees were simultaneously performing their core job functions and engaging in speech that involved content that would be highly protected by the First Amendment if it had been uttered by a private citizen. If a government employee suffered an adverse employment action as a result of such speech, was this a First Amendment issue? *Garcetti* has particular significance for current debates over the regulation of classroom speech, and in that case the Court put a large thumb on the scale in favor of the government.

Like *Connick*, *Garcetti* involved internal communications in a district attorney's office. The key issue in *Garcetti* was whether those internal communications, here a memo regarding the disposition of a case being handled by the office, passed the initial threshold of the *Pickering* test and involved speech in which the employee had a First Amendment interest.[10] Unlike *Connick*, the memo in *Garcetti* did not deal with a matter of only "personal interest" but rather with the substantive public business with which the office routinely dealt. Although the memo in question addressed matters of public interest, the Court concluded that the deputy district attorney was not speaking "as a citizen" in writing the memo to his superiors.

He was doing his job. Unlike Pickering's letter to the editor or the speech suppressed in the anti-subversive cases, the internal office memo was not promoting an "informed, vibrant dialogue in a democratic society."[11]

The *Garcetti* Court accepted that some "speech within the office" can receive constitutional protection, as can "some expressions related to the speaker's job." But the Court thought the distinguishing feature of the deputy district attorney's memo was that it was "made pursuant to his duties." He was speaking "as a prosecutor" in writing the memo, not as a citizen, and the memo "owes its existence to a public employee's professional responsibilities." It was speech "commissioned or created" by the employer. The employee was performing "the tasks he was paid to perform." Even if the content of the memo addressed a matter of public concern, it was outside the scope of First Amendment protection because it was made "pursuant to official responsibilities."[12]

Garcetti thus added to the threshold question in evaluating government employee speech. To receive greater constitutional protection, the employee must not only be speaking about a matter of public concern but must also be speaking in their private capacity as a citizen.

On its face *Garcetti* is debilitating to many academic freedom claims in state universities. The core protections of academic freedom involve speech that is part of a professor's "professional responsibilities," namely their teaching and scholarship. But the Court added an important proviso to its holding in *Garcetti*. In dissent, Justice David Souter highlighted the potential implications and added, "I have to hope that today's majority does not mean to imperil First Amendment protection of academic freedom in public colleges and universities, whose teachers necessarily speak and write 'pursuant to official duties.'"[13] In response, Justice Anthony Kennedy writing for the Court added that academic freedom cases might be different and "We need not, and for that reason do not, decide whether the analysis we conduct today would apply in the same manner to a case involving speech related to scholarship or teaching."[14]

This was no pro forma acknowledgment of the specific facts at hand in *Garcetti*. In an earlier case, Kennedy had pointed to the importance of the anti-subversive cases in establishing the critical principle that the danger of the state chilling "individual thought and expression" was "especially real in the University setting, where the State acts against a background and tradition of thought and experiment that is at the center of our intellectual and philosophical tradition."[15] In *Garcetti* itself, Kennedy explicitly recognized the "additional constitutional interests" in "expression related to academic scholarship or classroom instruction." The Court's "customary employee-speech jurisprudence" did not fully take into account those academic freedom interests and thus should be applied especially cautiously in the university setting.[16]

Even so, Kennedy's language in *Garcetti* has left the courts uncertain as to how to treat academic freedom claims and the professional speech of state university professors. Many courts have suggested that there is an academic freedom "exception" to the general rule laid down in *Garcetti*, but have struggled with how to understand the implications of any such exception. Others have questioned whether there is any genuine academic freedom exception to the general *Garcetti* rule at all. To those judges, the *Garcetti* rule applies to professors in the same way that it applies to any other government employee – any speech or writing that a professor engages in as part of his official duties is outside of the protection of the First Amendment. When a professor writes a memo to her chair, teaches a class or mentors a student, or produces scholarly research, she is engaging in speech that "owes its existence to a public employee's professional responsibilities" and she can claim no valid First Amendment interest in that speech.

A critical question, therefore, is how *Pickering* and *Garcetti* should be applied to legislative regulation of academic speech in state universities. Such regulations would force courts to confront precisely the question that the *Garcetti* Court bracketed. Professorial speech in the classroom is certainly an example of speech made pursuant to the professor's official responsibilities and as part of a task that a professor is paid to perform. When speaking in class, a professor is speaking as a professor, that is as a government employee, and not as a citizen. The substantive content of classroom speech might well be, and generally is, about matters of public concern, but *Garcetti*, at least without its reservation regarding academic freedom, tells us that is not enough to give government employee speech constitutional protection.

Academic Freedom and Government Employees

How then should *Pickering* and *Garcetti* be understood in the context of classroom speech? I argue that academic speech should be understood to be an exception to the *Garcetti* framework. *Garcetti* can only be reconciled with *Keyishian* if we understand that the particular kind of speech that professors are employed to engage in as part of their job responsibilities is speech that is of "special concern to the First Amendment."[17] By engaging in speech *as a professor*, these particular government employees are engaging in speech that is sheltered by the First Amendment, even though that is not true in the case of other government employees speaking in their role as employees. From a First Amendment perspective, professors speaking in class are differently situated than a district attorney writing a memo or a police officer speaking to a crowd or a public health officer releasing a statement about an infectious disease or a bus driver speaking to bus passengers. In order to create a workable doctrine regarding classroom speech, however, it is important to understand both the reasons why this form of speech as an employee should receive protection and how that protection can be appropriately delimited in a way that is consistent with the Court's concerns in both *Garcetti* and *Keyishian*.

We should begin with why classroom speech is not like a disposition memorandum. Politicians tried to suppress professorial expression of radical ideas in the mid-twentieth century and of divisive ideas about race and gender now, precisely because such ideas speak to matters of public concern and are politically disfavored. The attempt to suppress them is not motivated by such ordinary workplace concerns as insuring that universities operate efficiently but rather by broad political motivations regarding what ideas politicians believe are most compatible with a good society. The desire to censor such ideas on campus is the same as the desire to censor such ideas in the public sphere more broadly. This was particularly evident in the case of the anti-subversive legislation, when regulations of professorial speech were of a piece with regulations of speech more generally. As the Court's First Amendment jurisprudence gradually made it clear that radical ideas, as expressed by ordinary citizens, were constitutionally beyond the reach of politicians, the effort to suppress such speech by government employees lingered until the Court began to pare back those efforts as well.

In the early twenty-first century, it is clear that "critical race theory" or "divisive concepts" cannot be erased from the public sphere by government decree. No matter how much politicians might wish to suppress dangerous ideas shouted from a soapbox on a public sidewalk, modern First Amendment jurisprudence ties their hands. As a consequence, politicians have generally focused more narrowly on domains where they think they might have more constitutional leeway – government agencies, public schools, public libraries, and perhaps state universities. The government's interest in censoring speech about divisive concepts in higher education raises all the familiar concerns with censorship broadly that the Court has systematically rejected since the early years of the twentieth century. Suppressing divisive concepts in higher education does not look like the normal work of an employer managing the workplace but instead raises Justice Hugo Black's specter of "a transient majority" trying "to select the idea people can think about."[18] The state's interest in suppressing a professor's speech in this context is "not significantly greater than its interest in limiting a similar contribution by any member of the general public."[19]

The Court in *Connick* and *Garcetti* warned against the constitutionalization of workplace grievances. Judges should not be in the business of second-guessing a government employee's supervisor over how their work should be performed. Legislative bans on "critical race theory" do not look like ordinary workplace management, but rather look like political efforts to prevent the public from hearing about ideas that incumbent politicians do not like. Significantly, the effort to suppress speech on divisive concepts in university classrooms does not come from workplace managers at all. It is not the university officials who generally oversee the implementation of the curriculum or address teaching problems who are attempting to manage a faculty member by responding to the content of their classroom lectures. It is not department chairs or even deans who are moved to address abuses of the classroom in order to insure that educational services are properly and efficiently provided to students. It is the distant legislature overriding ordinary workplace managers in order to impose preventative bans on politically disfavored ideas. Allowing such legislative restrictions on classroom speech to stand would be anomalous within modern First Amendment jurisprudence.

Protecting academic speech from the undue influence of politicians is close to the heart of why the Court responded to the anti-subversive legislation of the postwar period by recognizing a constitutional interest in academic freedom in the first place. It was not because professors had unusually interesting things to say when opining in public about matters far distant from their scholarly expertise that the justices in the mid-twentieth century took a particular interest in universities. It was the need to protect free inquiry in scholarship and the classroom that the *Keyishian* Court concluded that "[o]ur Nation is deeply committed to safeguarding academic freedom."[20] It is because of teaching and scholarship that the university was a "center of independent thought."[21] It is in the context of teaching and scholarship that Justice Douglas worried about "a deadening dogma" taking the "place of free inquiry."[22] The "intellectual life of a university" is centrally focused on its academic endeavors. In laying down constitutional protections for academic freedom, the justices returned again and again to the importance of free inquiry in the classroom. "Teachers and students must always remain free to inquire, to study and to evaluate, to gain new maturity and understanding," Chief Justice Warren cautioned in the midst of the Second Red Scare, "otherwise our civilization will stagnate and die." Most obviously, the important *Sweezy* case was centered in part on a political investigation of the content of a lecture to a college class, an area in which the Court thought the "government should be extremely reticent to tread."[23] Universities do many things, but at the heart of a university's mission is the effort to advance, preserve, and communicate knowledge. Fulfilling that valuable mission requires freedom of thought.[24]

The Court thought there was a First Amendment interest in academic speech because they thought such speech involved the public interest. How broad or narrow the audience for a particular example of professorial speech should not be a salient factor in determining whether the content of that speech involves a matter of public concern under *Pickering*. In the context of scholarly communication, matters of public concern are probably most analogous to the Court's approach to obscenity and whether a given expression has "serious literary, artistic, political, or scientific value."[25] Scholars seek to add to the storehouse of human knowledge, and it is the public interest in filling that storehouse with as much truthful knowledge as possible that makes academic speech distinctively a matter of public concern. Esoteric literary criticism or technical scientific analysis has comparable constitutional value for academic freedom purposes as applied ethics or political theory. The speech in most university classrooms does not resemble the kind of political argumentation found in Marvin Pickering's letter, but it is of public concern nonetheless. From the perspective of *Keyishian*, it would be equally alarming if the state attempted to suppress frequentist statistical analyses because it favored Bayesianism or suppress Keynesian economic theory because it favored monetarist economic theory, even though most members of the general public have no familiarity with either school of thought.

A year after *Pickering*, the Court said, "it is the purpose of the First Amendment to preserve an uninhibited marketplace of ideas in which truth will ultimately prevail."[26] As the AAUP declared in their joint statement of principles with the Association of American Colleges in 1940, "institutions of higher education are conducted for the common good," which in turn "depends upon the free search for truth and its free exposition."[27] Whether that search for truth involves trying to understand the furthest reaches of the universe, the meaning of ancient burial rituals, the conditions of war and peace, or the effects of race on social relations, it is necessarily a matter of public concern and of relevance to the First Amendment and its values. If the very purpose of the First Amendment is to hold open the search for truth against those who would seek to obstruct it, preserving free inquiry across the university is imperative.

Academic speech is by design communicative to a broad audience. That is not to say that it is necessarily accessible to or of interest to a mass audience. Most academic speech is highly specialized and is fortunate if it attracts the attention of even a specialized audience. But it is central to the academic enterprise to disseminate knowledge to others. Teachers in the classroom are seeking to impart knowledge to a body of students. Scholars producing scholarship have a responsibility to share the fruits of their research with others, whether those others are expert scholars or members of the mass public. Academic speech is concerned not only with advancing and preserving knowledge but also with disseminating it. Distinctively, academic speech is done in public and before an audience in a way that is quite distant from a lawyer writing a memo for his supervisor and in a way that distinguishes it from the kind of "expressions made at work" that could be found in most governmental or non-governmental offices. The Court in *Garcetti* noted that whether speech took place in public or in the office is not "dispositive" for the question of whether it is protected by the First Amendment, but the more speech resembles speech in public the more credibly it is the type of expression that merits First Amendment protection.

Certainly there are examples of speech that are part of a professor's job responsibilities that do more closely resemble the kind of speech at issue in *Connick* and *Garcetti*. Like other employees, professors write memoranda, reports, performance evaluations, and the like, and such speech that is comparable to generic employee speech is traditionally understood to fall outside the scope of even contractual academic freedom protections. While there are border cases of various sorts, generally speaking the more professorial speech resembles the kind of speech that is routinely found in non-academic workspaces the less the justification for treating it as academic speech that is special under the First Amendment.[28]

The Court in *Connick* clarified that constitutional protections for government employee speech depended on the "content, form and context of a given statement." The content of academic speech is generally a matter of public concern, but *Connick* and *Garcetti* tell us that is not sufficient. Academic speech also has a form and context, however, that places it closer to traditional public speech.

Recognizing academic speech as constitutionally protected is not without challenges. In particular, the courts should still want to avoid being drawn into what are essentially workplace grievances, even when those grievances involve academic speech. The central concern of the academic freedom cases culminating in *Keyishian* and of *Pickering* balancing of government employee speech is to insulate academic speech from outside political influence. It is the political imposition of dogma and orthodoxy that is of constitutional concern. Courts have, quite reasonably, taken a highly deferential approach to claims that reduce to disagreements about the scholarly merits of faculty hiring and promotion cases, for example. "The courts will not serve as a Super-Tenure Review Committee."[29] It would be an error to adopt a constitutional standard that invites judicial oversight of how such internal academic affairs are resolved.

In the context of a state university, academic speech by professors made "pursuant to official duties" should be understood to be constitutionally protected. For most government employees, *Garcetti* holds the opposite, that employee speech loses constitutional protection precisely because it has been specifically commissioned by a governmental employer. But professors are employed to perform an unusual and specific role, a role that is close to the heart of the constitutional enterprise. They are employed, in part, to produce and disseminate the kind of ideas that are of public interest and that the First Amendment is understood to safeguard. Recognizing that government employee speech crosses that threshold does not end the judicial inquiry. A court would still need to consider how to balance the First Amendment interest against the government employer's legitimate interests in managing the workplace, but the judiciary's constitutional scrutiny of legislative restrictions on university classroom speech should not be stopped at the threshold.[30]

Academic speech that professors are "paid to perform" comes with its own limits. Professors are paid to perform constitutionally protected speech, but not all professorial speech is what universities have commissioned. Such speech might better be regarded as private speech and not academic speech at all. That is, some things professors say while "on the job" and in the workplace are not examples of them speaking "as a professor" but rather are examples of them speaking "as a private citizen." On such occasions, the First Amendment interest of the professor might be quite limited.

When professors are engaging in academic speech in the context of scholarship or teaching, the First Amendment interest in protecting such speech is particularly high. The question then becomes what legitimate interests the state has in regulating such speech and how weighty are those interests. There are circumstances in which the state has recognizable interests in managing classroom speech. The university can set the curriculum and can expect that professorial speech in the classroom will be both germane to that curriculum and professionally competent. When, however, professorial speech in the classroom is both germane and professionally competent, the state's legitimate interest in sanctioning professors for such speech is quite low.

Viewpoint-based discrimination by state officials far removed from the disciplinary authorities best situated to assess academic speech should be especially suspect. It is one thing for state officials to determine that a given university will concentrate its offerings on the sciences and not the humanities or will be home to a law school but not a medical school. It is quite another thing for state officials to command that some ideas in the humanities or some legal theories be banished from the classroom or that students may be introduced to some theses but may not be allowed to hear contrary arguments and evidence. If a legislature were to direct that a state university establish a law school but then decree that the law school must not hire any faculty who advocate for originalist theories of constitutional interpretation, or allow any professor to teach a law-and-economics perspective on antitrust law, it would be engaged in a constitutionally troubling effort to restrict scholarly discourse and delimit the ideas that law students are allowed to consider and understand. Rather than nurturing a marketplace of ideas, the state would be seeking to hobble the scholarly pursuit of the truth and debase the quality of education to be provided.

Setting Some Guardrails on Classroom Speech

Traditional principles of academic freedom are understood to be qualified, not absolute. In the particular context of classroom speech, faculty speech is delimited by requirements of germaneness and professional competence. The AAUP's Statement of Principles nods to the germaneness condition by noting that teachers "should be careful not to introduce into their teaching controversial matter which has no relation to their subject."[31] A teacher in a classroom has a captive audience of students, which creates a responsibility on the part of the teacher not to abuse that captive audience with irrelevant remarks. Teachers are given a privileged platform in a classroom for a particular purpose. From the student's perspective, their time is not to be frittered away with speech that is irrelevant to the educational purpose of the class nor are they to be hijacked into the service of the professor's pet personal causes. From the university's perspective, the professional duty that a teacher is to perform is to instruct students in the subject matter of the class. Teachers who spend their time in the classroom doing something else are not performing their professional duty, and as a consequence can be reasonably sanctioned by the university for that malfeasance.

Courts have found the germaneness standard useful for assessing how much protection classroom speech should receive, and they have had to make similar judgments in adjudicating other types of legal claims. In *Kracunas v. Iona College*, for example, the Second Circuit Court of Appeals emphasized that "conduct shown to be harassment (as opposed to teaching)" could appropriately be sanctioned. Although the college raised academic freedom concerns that might arise from administrative monitoring of how professors interact with students as they perform their duties, the court thought that at least in this case both university officials and judges could assess evidence of whether professorial conduct "was done in good faith as part of his teaching . . . [or could] reasonably be seen as appropriate to further a pedagogical purpose." Classroom speech that served a pedagogical purpose was entitled to legal protection, but speech that did not could be appropriately proscribed.[32] In another sexual harassment case involving "classroom language," the Sixth Circuit made use of the university's own harassment policy, which recognized that "speech in the classroom which is germane to course content is not subject to this policy." The "unique context" of "a classroom where a college professor is speaking to a captive audience of students" both raised the threat of professors abusing their positions to harass their students and served as a "unique milieu . . . where debate and the class of viewpoints are encouraged – if not necessary – to spur intellectual growth." Where classroom speech "was found to serve the purpose of advancing viewpoints, however repugnant" or "had as their purpose influencing or informing public debate," then it merited substantial constitutional protection. The governmental employer's interest in regulating professorial classroom speech that is not "germane to course content" is much higher.[33] "[G]ratuitous in-class" speech is of a different constitutional nature than speech that is a legitimate part of "an academic discussion."[34]

It should be noted that one circuit court has recently suggested that germaneness to course content should not be deemed relevant to determining what professorial classroom speech is constitutionally protected. A panel of the Sixth Circuit resolved a case involving a public university's pronoun policy as applied to a professor's classroom speech. In doing so, the court rejected the claim that there was no "academic-freedom exception to *Garcetti*" and that governmental employers had a free hand to regulate professorial classroom speech. The court thought the thrust of the Supreme Court's decisions growing out of the anti-subversive controversies had established that "a professor's in-class speech to his students is anything but speech by an ordinary government employee." The "need for the free exchange of ideas in the college classroom is unlike that in other public workplace settings." The court was emphatic that

> public universities do not have a license to act as classroom thought police. They cannot force professors to avoid controversial viewpoints altogether in deference to a state-mandated orthodoxy. Otherwise, our public universities could transform the next generation of leaders into "closed-circuit recipients of only that which the State chooses to communicate."[35]

So far, so good.

At one point, however, the court characterized that academic freedom exception as covering "all classroom speech related to matters of public concern, whether that speech is germane to the contents of the lecture or not." It is not clear that the court thought the germaneness issue was relevant to resolving the case before it, and the court never explicitly referred to germaneness beyond this brief mention. The court specifically noted that "some classroom speech falls outside the [*Garcetti* academic freedom] exception," including "non-ideological ministerial" speech that professors might be called upon to make in the classroom. Moreover, the court was also concerned with arguing that the instructor's selection of pronouns to be used in the classroom conveyed a salient "message." This particular case involved a philosophy professor teaching courses on political philosophy, ethics, and the history of Christian thought, and the university's directives extended to restricting the professor from stating his views on the pronoun policy in his course syllabus. The court also thought that the professor's speech had not "inhibited his duties in the classroom."[36] The court's extension of the academic freedom exception to classroom speech whether or not "that speech is germane" is not clearly rooted in the broader jurisprudence regarding academic freedom, was not specifically explained or justified by the court, and may not have been necessary to resolving this particular case.

Casting aside a germaneness requirement risks tying the hands of university officials to address problems with how professors treat their captive audience and even with whether they are performing their core duties, which do not primarily include sharing with students in class the professor's "core religious and philosophical beliefs." Such a move should not be necessary to resolving the main issues associated with the recent divisive concepts policies either, since in many cases they would implicate classroom speech that *is* germane to the subject matter of the course. Whether university officials, or state legislatures, could reasonably take action against professors who unnecessarily introduce into their classes controversial content that is not germane to their subject matter can be put off to another day. That is to say, there may be important constitutional differences between critical race theory being discussed in a chemistry class and in an African American studies class.

A second condition on professorial speech in the classroom is that it be professionally competent. The professional duty of the instructor in the classroom is to provide professionally competent instruction. That is the type of speech professors are commissioned to perform, and it is the type of speech both students and university officials can reasonably expect to receive. It is entailed within the scope of academic freedom that a professor might introduce students to radical, marginal, or not widely accepted ideas, but an instructor has a responsibility to insure that students recognize the context of those ideas and how they fit within the broader body of knowledge. A professor who routinely presented to students as mainstream and correct ideas that are in fact roundly rejected by experts in the field, or a professor who routinely conveys a false understanding of what the state of knowledge within a field of study might be, is not conducting themselves in a professionally competent manner. Academic freedom has value to the extent that it protects professionally competent speech. If it instead becomes a mechanism for shielding instructors peddling proverbial snake oil to their students, then it serves no social function. A civil engineering professor who teaches students in such a way that bridges that they build would fall down rather than stay upright is not protected by academic freedom. Universities could reasonably sanction professors for indulging in such classroom speech without raising constitutional concerns.[37]

Professional competence both conditions and underwrites protections for academic freedom. The founding statement of the American Association of University Professors, the 1915 Declaration of Principles, called for greater security of tenure in order to give scholars and teachers the independence necessary to engage in free inquiry without fear of reprisal for reaching unpopular or inconvenient conclusions. The AAUP recognized, however, that "there can be no rights without corresponding duties." It is only those "who carry on their work in the temper of the scientific inquirer who may justify this claim" to freedom of teaching. A professor who seeks to indoctrinate rather than teach cannot legitimately hide behind a claim of a freedom to teach. In the words of that 1915 Declaration, "his business is not to provide his students with ready-made conclusions, but to train them to think for themselves, and to provide them with access to those materials which they need if they are to think intelligently." A professor who fails in that task should not be sheltered from discipline, and, "if this profession should prove itself unwilling to purge its ranks of the incompetent and the unworthy, or to prevent the freedom which it claims in the name of science from being used as a shelter for inefficiency, for superficiality, or for uncritical and intemperate partisanship, it is certain that the task will be performed by others."[38]

In responding to the anti-subversive push of the McCarthy era, the AAUP laid out what should qualify as good cause to terminate a member of the faculty. "Action against a faculty member cannot rightly be taken on grounds that limit his freedom as an individual, as a member of the academic community, or as a teacher and scholar." Terminating a professor's employment merely for engaging in politically unpopular speech, whether in the classroom or in scholarship, is hardly consistent with such an aspiration. Removal from the faculty merely for being a member of the Communist Party, for example, would violate those principles. "Removal can be justified only on the ground, established by evidence, of unfitness to teach because of incompetence, lack of scholarly objectivity or integrity, serious misuse of the classroom or of academic prestige, gross personal misconduct, or conscious participation in conspiracy against the government."[39] Professionally competent speech merits protection, even if it is unpopular or controversial. Professionally incompetent speech merits sanction, even if it is popular or conformist.

The First Amendment scholar Robert Post highlighted the point that professional competence is not only a standard that the individual faculty member must meet and that the profession must enforce. It is also a standard that government officials cannot appropriately abrogate. "We should expect," he notes, "to see First Amendment coverage triggered whenever government seeks by . . . legislation to disrupt the communication of accurate expert knowledge." He observes that courts have rebuffed legislation that requires, for example, medical providers "to give untruthful, misleading and irrelevant information to patients."[40] Such governmental requirements that professional speech be incompetent so as to better satisfy political sensibilities implicates First Amendment rights.[41] As one court noted, "the State cannot compel an individual simply to speak the State's ideological message," though it can reasonably require professionals to convey "truthful" and "relevant" information.[42] The Supreme Court has recently pointed out, "as with other kinds of speech, regulating the content of professionals' speech 'pose[s] the inherent risk that the Government seeks not to advance a legitimate regulatory goal, but to suppress unpopular ideas or information.'"[43] Whether the state compels a professional to communicate information that the professional community believes is untrue or prohibits a professional from communicating information that the professional community believes is true, the result is that the state is substituting its own ideological commitments for the free pursuit of truth by the relevant experts. For the state to require professorial speech in the classroom to be incompetent, whether by omission or commission, would vitiate the value that academic freedom under the First Amendment is intended to provide to society.

Professorial classroom speech that is neither germane to the class nor professionally competent is deserving of little constitutional protection. Note, however, that such speech might still be on matters of public concern. A chemistry professor who spends his class time talking about the presidential election or a medical professor who instructs his class that vaccines cause autism might well be engaging in speech that in other circumstances would be entitled to robust constitutional protection. A professor who indulges in such speech on their private blog on their own time would enjoy some presumptive protection under *Pickering*.[44] A professor who engages in such speech in the classroom, however, would appropriately be subject to adverse employment action.

How Does a Constitutionally Bounded Academic Freedom Work in Practice?

We can imagine four separate scenarios of professorial speech in a state university to clarify how *Pickering*, *Garcetti*, and the constitutionalized protection for academic freedom referenced in *Keyishian* would interact. The examples demonstrate how the three cases can be reconciled to simultaneously protect free inquiry into controversial ideas in a university setting and the efficient functioning of a university as a particular kind of state agency.

When professors speak on campus, they might speak either *as a professor* or *as a citizen*. When they speak as a citizen, standard *Pickering* analysis for free expression applies as to whether the speech is about a matter of public concern or disruptive to the functioning of the university. When they speak as a professor in performing their employment duties, academic freedom principles are paramount, but to place the speech under the broad protections of academic freedom we must ask whether the speech is both germane and professionally competent.

Scenario 1: A law-school professor teaching a class on race and American law conducts a classroom discussion of core ideas associated with the scholarly literature on critical race theory and in the process distributes class materials and advocates ideas that run afoul of legislative proposals curtailing the introduction of divisive concepts into university classes.

Such classroom speech would fall squarely within the domain of speech made pursuant to official duties. But for an academic freedom exception, *Garcetti* would allow government officials to suppress such speech. A proper academic freedom exception, however, would recognize such speech as robustly protected under *Keyishian*. The divisive concepts bills would be a viewpoint discriminatory interference with constitutionally protected speech, which should weigh heavily in favor of the professor. Indeed, the anti-critical race theory bills look like precisely the kind of prior restraint through "sweeping statutory impediment to speech" that the Court has said is particularly disfavored even within a government employment context.[45]

If a court were to engage in a balancing exercise as suggested by the *Pickering* framework, the government would have a heavy burden to bear in demonstrating that a statutory prior restraint on the expression of certain viewpoints in a university classroom is justified. The professor in this scenario is engaging in professionally competent speech appropriate to the subject matter of the course. By attempting to restrain professors from engaging in such speech, the state legislature would not simply be attempting to specify the curriculum of the university. It would be attempting to legislate what can be said when teaching that curriculum. The state would be authorizing teaching certain course content, but it would also be demanding an orthodoxy on how that content is understood. Professors are free to discuss controversies regarding race, but only if they toe the legislature's line on how those controversies are to be viewed. It is precisely such an imposition of orthodoxy in higher education that the Court regarded as repugnant to the Constitution.

Scenario 2: A law-school professor teaching a class on contracts regularly spends large portions of the class time discussing recent political events and hosting guest lecturers to advocate for the professor's favored political causes.

Such classroom speech is not made *pursuant* to official duties since no professor is employed for the purpose of sharing political opinions with a captive audience of students to the exclusion of the course material that students are supposed to be learning. It does, however, take advantage of the privileged access to the student's time that a professor has as a consequence of his state employment. Lecturing to students is "within the scope of an employee's duties,"[46] but lecturing to students about his personal political beliefs is not.

The content of such private speech does involve "commenting upon matters of public concern," however, and *Pickering* would suggest that it would be necessary "to arrive at a balance between the interests of the teacher, as a citizen . . . and the interest of the State, as an employer, in promoting the efficiency of the public services it performs through its employees." However, the timing and circumstances of such speech weighs heavily in favor of the state as an employer restricting it. *Pickering* itself emphasized that a letter to the editor of a newspaper could not "be presumed to have in any way . . . impeded the teacher's proper performance of his daily duties."[47] Departing from assigned duties in order to engage in private political speech, on the other hand, implicates the need of the public employer to "be able to control the operations of its workplace."[48] It matters not whether students or school officials share the political opinions that the professor is espousing in this case. A germaneness test is neutral as to the viewpoint being expressed in the speech at issue. Whether a radical or a reactionary, the professor is expected to discuss contract law in class, not politics. A state university employer has a strong interest in preventing a professor from imposing on a captive audience of students speech "with no academic purpose or justification."[49] A germaneness test for professorial classroom speech distinguishes between the kind of speech that is properly protected by the First Amendment concerns raised by *Keyishian* and the kind of speech that interferes with the delivery of the public services that the state has an interest in maintaining.

Scenario 3: A political science professor teaching a class on campaigns and elections in American politics dedicates the semester to expounding on his belief that Italian defense firms use satellites to change American vote tallies, that Venezuela manipulates American voting machines, and that North Korea smuggles into American ballot boxes counterfeit paper ballots produced in China.

Unlike the private speech at issue in Scenario 2, the classroom speech in this situation is indeed pursuant to the professor's duties. The professor is commissioned to lecture to students about how elections operate in the United States, and that is what the professor is doing. The trouble is that the professor is performing those duties in an incompetent fashion by conveying to students ideas that are roundly rejected within the relevant expert community and conveying them as if they enjoyed scholarly validity.

The state's interest in excluding such speech from the class-room is just as real, even though it bears a closer relationship to the kind of speech the academic freedom cases are concerned with protecting. Even when government employee speech merits First Amendment protection, the government still has an "employer's legitimate interest[] in its mission."[50] The core mission of the university is truth-seeking, which it advances by nurturing a scholarly community capable of building up expert knowledge through a process of inquiry governed by discipli-nary norms and ways of testing and evaluating claims. Both the field of accepted knowledge and the modes of proceeding in advancing knowledge are subject to change within a vibrant scholarly enterprise. Ideas that were once accepted get rejected over time. Modes of inquiry that were once taken seriously get discarded as unreliable. Academia gives a great deal of leeway to individual scholars to test those boundaries on the assumption that fields of scholarly inquiry should always hold themselves open to legitimate challenge. But there are still limits, and a great deal of scholarly activity is expended in evaluating the quality of research and of scholars and making determinations about what to embrace and what to reject. Those limits are particularly pertinent in the classroom setting, where students are not in a position to evaluate whether they are being provided with mainstream or idiosyncratic ideas and professors have a particular responsibility to be clear with students when they introduce them to more controversial material.

Scholarly assessments of the substantive quality of scholarly writing and teaching have always been accepted as consistent with academic freedom principles. A key consideration is who is making such an assessment. The AAUP has long emphasized that academic freedom is endangered if such judgments are made by non-scholars, whether legislators or boards of trustees. "The proper fulfillment of the work of the professoriate requires that our universities shall be so free that no fair-minded person shall find any excuse for even a suspicion that the utterances of university teachers are shaped or restricted by the judgment, not of professional scholars, but of inexpert and possibly not wholly disinterested persons outside of their ranks."[51] Even when fellow scholars are making such judgments, we might still worry that scholarly assessments can become a mere pretext for exercising power for inappropriate ends, whether racial or sexual discrimination or political hostility. Academic freedom principles do not exclude the need for such basic judgments of whether to confer a scholarly degree on a student or whether to employ or promote a potential member of the faculty.

In the specific context of government employee speech, courts have likewise recognized that the need to make such judgments weighs in the balance on the side of governmental

interests. When engaged in a *Pickering* balancing of interests, courts have noted that even constitutionally protected
employee speech might "reflect upon the employee's competence to perform his or her job."[52] Government employers
are "entirely justified" in "evaluating the soundness" of an
employee's speech when that speech is relevant to their job
functions. Determining whether an employee displays "a
lack of professional competence" is an unavoidable aspect of
the government acting in its role as an employer, and that
need does not evaporate when the speech in question occurs
in a classroom setting or has First Amendment relevance.[53]
"Classroom performance" is within the scope of an employer's
interest.[54] Even given robust First Amendment protection for
academic freedom, state universities retain the ability to dismiss the historian of twentieth-century European history who
insists on instructing his students that the Holocaust is a myth
or the astronomer who requires his students to learn that the
sun revolves around the earth.[55]

Scenario 4: A group of professors eating lunch in a faculty
lounge on campus get into a spirited discussion about the role
of race in American society in which one loudly proclaims the
truth of ideas banned by legislation aimed at excluding divisive
concepts from higher education. A portion of the conversation
is recorded by a passing student and posted on social media,
resulting in demands from state political leaders that the professor be fired.

Such a case falls neatly within a traditional *Pickering* framework. Although the speech at issue here takes place on the job
site rather than in an extramural context, the speech is clearly
private and not part of the ordinary duties of the job of a professor. The professor in this context is acting as a citizen, not as
a government employee. Moreover, the speech relates to matters of public concern, and thus passes the threshold question
of whether they are entitled to constitutional consideration.

The question then becomes whether the state *as an employer* has a sufficiently weighty countervailing interest in restricting such speech. Private remarks in ordinary workplace conversations diminish the state's interest in regulating such speech unless it directly "interfered with the efficient functioning of the office."[56] The faculty lounge is recognized as a place "where professors regularly talk about political and social issues with one another" and where the state employer's interest in regulating the content of the ideas expressed is quite limited.[57] The fact that the speech was to a small audience and "inhouse" might be "considered in determining whether the speech addressed a matter of public concern," but it does not in itself heighten the state's legitimate interest in punishing such speech.[58]

Of course, professorial speech cannot always be so neatly categorized. The first step is knowing whether a professor is speaking in a context that is pursuant to the professor's employment duties or not, that is whether the professor is speaking as a professor or as a citizen. When a professor stands before an assigned class of students during a class period, the distinction is fairly straightforward. Matters might be somewhat more complicated if the professor is standing in the classroom before a class is scheduled to begin or is meeting with students in her office. Surely not every interaction between professors and students is best understood as pursuant to their job responsibilities. Professors mentor and advise students informally, but professors also interact with students in a variety of situations that are not properly speaking part of the job. A professor who pauses at a campus rally while walking to class is not performing their employment function, but a student who consults with a professor during office hours is eliciting professional speech from the faculty member.

The boundaries between germane and non-germane speech and professionally competent and professionally incompetent speech are likewise sometimes fuzzy. Some academic disciplines have relatively well-defined boundaries regarding their subject matter, but others might be much more capacious such that it is less clear what topics might not be germane to a given class discussion. A lecture on early nineteenth century American literature might be expected to roam further afield than a lecture on thermodynamics. Allowances must likewise be made for speech that is non-germane from a subject matter perspective but that is apposite from a pedagogical perspective. Professors who tell jokes to help build community and sustain interest might be engaging in speech that is non-germane when taken in isolation but that makes sense in context. Professors pushing such boundaries no doubt owe the students an obligation not to be unnecessarily controversial. Jokes, asides, illustrations, and analogies should not themselves become a source of tension. A professor who "livens up" his lectures with a running series of acerbic political comments is not off the hook for introducing unnecessarily controversial material into the class simply because he finds his own remarks witty, just as courts have not been impressed with professors who aver that their sexually lewd remarks or crude language in class are just part of their teaching technique. Education is a social endeavor and professors cannot be expected to robotically stick to a script, but frequent digressions into tangential topics of conversation risk crossing the boundaries of academic freedom, especially when those digressions are contentious.

Whether a particular example of classroom speech is professionally competent might also not have a clear-cut answer. The social sciences and the humanities tend to be far more internally fragmented than the natural sciences. It might be relatively easy to tell whether a chemist is doing something that is recognizable as professionally competent chemistry. It can be much harder to reach agreement on how academic work in philosophy or sociology should be conducted. The accepted ways of knowing in political science are both varied and sharply contested. The *wissenschaft* of a particular discipline might be only loosely rather than tightly constrained. Such diversity emphasizes the importance of being guided by the local experts, by a professor's disciplinary peers. The outside observer – whether a judge or a dean – might suppose that a professor's classroom flights of fancy transcend the bounds of professional competence, but the professor's peers might see the logic of it. The protections of academic freedom should not depend on whether outsiders understand and agree with how an academic discipline is constructed and pursued. Provosts and trustees might take such concerns into account when deciding whether to invest more resources into a particular field of study, but professors should enjoy the protections of academic freedom while pursuing the activities that are recognized as meaningful and competent within their own discipline.

Pickering is most helpful in thinking about government employee speech that does not involve the employee's duties as an employee. When a professor is speaking "as a citizen," whether outside the workplace or even in the workplace, then the *Pickering* framework usefully identifies the considerations at play when governmental employers attempt to sanction such speech. It is less helpful, however, in identifying when speech should be protected or what considerations ought to be relevant to the employer's actions when a professor is performing his or her duties as a professor. *Garcetti* establishes that government employees outside the educational context have few First Amendment rights when performing their duties, but provides little guidance for the educational context. *Garcetti* raises the question, but does not answer it, of how the courts should address First Amendment claims raised by professorial speech that is pursuant to their official duties.

When grappling with the anti-subversive legislation of the mid-twentieth century, the Court came to appreciate the extent to which the speech that professors routinely engage in as part of their academic duties, in both their scholarly activities and in the classroom, is central to the First Amendment. The Court cannot now allow state legislatures to restrict the set of ideas professors are allowed to discuss in the classroom or the viewpoint that professors adopt relative to those ideas without repudiating those hard-won lessons.

Where most government employees enjoy their greatest constitutional protection when speaking in their private capacity *as citizens*, as the Court recognized in *Pickering*, university professors are distinctive in requiring constitutional protection for their speech *as government employees*. To effectuate the insight that academic freedom is "of special concern to the First Amendment," the Court would need to insulate classroom speech from legislative intrusions that serve a primary purpose of attempting to control what ideas are discussed and taken seriously in the public sphere.

The fact that some professors are government employees does not eliminate their First Amendment interest in being able to teach students ideas that may be controversial and out of favor with incumbent government officials but that are germane to their classes and within the realm of professional competence. The state has no distinctive interest *as an employer* in sanctioning such controversial but germane and professionally competent speech. When state officials take steps to suppress such speech, they are doing so not in their role as employers but in their role as regulators. And, relative to the government *as regulators*, the Court has emphasized that the First Amendment interest in developing, expressing, and deliberating on controversial ideas is exceedingly strong.

6

Teaching in the Government School

If we step back from considering the individual free-speech rights of government employees, we should also consider the nature of the public university as a governmental entity. The Court's government employee speech doctrine has empha- sized that government employees do not lose all of their First Amendment rights when they accept a job working for the government, just as the Court has also emphasized that public-school students do not lose all their First Amendment rights when they step inside the schoolhouse doors. But as we have seen, the Court has over time clarified that a gov- ernment employee's speech rights are much more limited when the employee is actually on the job and performing his duties. Supervisors in a government workplace need to be able to manage, and if necessary discipline, their employees if the workplace is to function smoothly, and the First Amendment does not require that government workplaces be dysfunctional.

I argued in the last chapter that this legitimate interest that the government has in maintaining a well-functioning work- place does not support political efforts to suppress disfavored speech in public university classrooms. Such efforts look much less like workplace management and much more like simple politically motivated censorship, and any meaningful First Amendment protection for academic freedom must be sturdy enough to shield the classroom from would-be censors. Legislative restrictions on university classroom discussion should not survive a *Pickering* analysis. Such classroom speech should cross the threshold of receiving First Amendment protection, and a professor's First Amendment interests should outweigh the government's interest in restricting speech in this context.

There is a second potential path by which divisive concepts bans might be constitutionally justified. The classroom speech of public university professors might be characterized as a form of government speech. The Court's doctrine relating to government employee speech has been concerned with identifying the speech rights of individual employees. Although related, the Court's doctrine regarding government speech has been concerned with identifying when speech in the public square should be understood to be the government's own messaging and with elaborating the constitutional rules that regulate that speech. Rather than thinking about the government regulating and restricting the speech of professors in university classrooms, we might instead think about the government conveying its own messages in university classrooms through the instrument of an employed professor. If divisive concepts and anti-critical race theory laws are doing the latter rather than the former, then a different set of constitutional considerations come into play.

In this chapter, I examine whether laws of this sort can appropriately be brought within the umbrella of government speech and pass constitutional muster on that basis. I argue that they should not. Not only would this use of government speech doctrine severely damage academic freedom protections in state universities, but it would be a misapplication of the Court's existing approach to identifying government speech. Classroom speech by public university professors is best understood as their own speech, not the government's speech. When the legislature tells professors what they can and cannot say in the classroom, the legislature is acting as a regulator attempting to censor speech and not as a government body attempting to engage in its own expressive activity.

The Government's Own Speech

The Court has made plain that the "Government's own speech . . . is exempt from First Amendment scrutiny."[1] When the government speaks with its own voice, it necessarily must make decisions based on the content and viewpoint of the substantive issues on which it chooses to speak. The government may legitimately favor some ideas and express disapproval of others when the government is engaged in its own speech. The government can tell its citizens that smoking is bad for their health, or that democracy is a good form of government. The government can proclaim that July 4, 1776 is a date worth celebrating, or that immigrants benefit the country. The First Amendment prevents the government from suppressing or disadvantaging disfavored ideas, but "it does not regulate government speech."[2]

The government can participate in the marketplace of ideas and advocate on behalf of its own favored ideas. It just cannot dictate to the citizenry that it must embrace the government's favored ideas or prevent the citizenry from hearing competing perspectives. Justice Antonin Scalia observed in a concurring opinion in a case involving government-funded art:

> It is the very business of government to favor and disfavor points of view on (in modern times, at least) innumerable subjects . . . And it makes not a bit of difference, insofar as either common sense or the Constitution is concerned, whether these officials further their (and, in a democracy, our) favored point of view

by achieving it directly (having government-employed artists paint pictures, for example, or government-employed doctors perform abortions); or by advocating it officially (establishing an Office of Art Appreciation, for example, or an Office of Voluntary Population Control); or by giving money to others who achieve or advocate it (funding private art classes, for example, or Planned Parenthood). None of this has anything to do with abridging anyone's speech.[3]

The curriculum of a public school might readily be understood to be an example of such government speech. The government creates the public schools, determines the curriculum, chooses the textbooks, and employs the teachers. When those teachers teach the curriculum in the classroom, they might not be speaking for themselves but are instead speaking on behalf of the government. Teachers might be the mere mouthpieces of the government and, if so, then the government necessarily has the right to determine what that mouthpiece will say. When government speech is at stake, the government might give positive direction so that certain ideas are expressed on its behalf, or it might set negative limits so that certain ideas are forbidden to be expressed on its behalf. Even as the Court recognized a First Amendment interest in resisting compelled speech in the Flag Salute Case, it admitted that "the State may 'require teaching by instruction and study of all in our history and in the structure and organization of our government, including the guaranties of civil liberty which tend to inspire patriotism and love of country.'"[4] California, for example, not only imposes requirements regarding the public-school curriculum, such as the directive that "instruction in the social sciences shall include . . . a study of the role and contributions" of myriad groups to the development of the state and the nation "with particular emphasis on portraying the role of these groups in contemporary society." It also prohibits some ideas from being included within the public-school curriculum, such as the directive that no school board may "adopt any instructional materials for use in the schools" that includes "any matter reflecting adversely upon persons on the basis of race or ethnicity, gender, religion, disability, nationality, or sexual orientation" or "any sectarian or denominational doctrine or propaganda contrary to law."[5] Through the apparatus of the public-school system "the state commands powerful machinery to prescribe and to instill basic values in politics, nationalism, and other matters of opinion."[6]

Giving the government free rein to convey its own messages nonetheless creates some First Amendment complications. The state may advance its "official view as to proper appreciation of history, state pride, and individualism," for example, in any number of ways, but it cannot dragoon a private individual into becoming "the courier for such [a] message."[7] Given the expansive scope of the modern government, however, it is not always obvious how to disentangle government speech from private speech. There is a particular risk that the government might use the government-speech doctrine "as a cover for censorship"[8] or as a "subterfuge for favoring certain private speakers over others based on viewpoint."[9] It thus becomes particularly important to determine, in the words of Justice Samuel Alito, "whether the government is actually expressing its own views, or the real speaker is a private party and the government is surreptitiously engaged in the 'regulation of private speech.'"[10]

The academic freedom exception to government employee speech explored in the last chapter complicates an easy resolution of the government speech problem. It is easier to distinguish between private speakers and government speakers when considering speech by government employees than when considering private speakers making use of government property. When a government employee engages in speech pursuant to their official duties and speaks as an employee, there is at least a prima facie expectation that the employee is speaking on behalf of the government. Government employee speech and government speech are largely reconciled by *Garcetti*'s emphasis on the employee's official responsibilities, but the academic freedom exception leaves that reconciliation incomplete in the educational context.

The lawyers for the state of Florida are clear about how they think that reconciliation should be accomplished. "The substance of the instruction and curriculum offered at public universities . . . is heartland government speech."[11] Indeed, many courts have concluded that "teachers hire out their own speech."[12] The speech of professors in public university classrooms might, therefore, simply be the speech of the government. Professors might be employed to convey the government's message, and nothing more. If so, they cannot object to the legislature telling them which messages it wants them to convey.

This is a sweeping and powerful claim. It is so sweeping, in fact, that there would be little room left over for academic freedom if it were to be adopted. The "pall of orthodoxy" would be a feature, not a bug, in a government school. Students might still have a First Amendment right to resist that orthodoxy, of course. The students may be free to criticize and reject the government's message or express alternative views of their own, but they would not be free to hear competing messages, at least not from the professor. The professor's job would be to say the words that their political bosses want them to say. State university professors would be, in John Dewey's vernacular, a "hired man."

This is, in fact, how courts have thought about public-school teachers. States like Florida hope that judges can be persuaded that state university professors are, constitutionally speaking, the same as middle-school teachers. Courts have thus far skirted the issue. Judge Frank Easterbrook, a former law professor at the University of Chicago, was typical when observing in a case involving the classroom speech of an elementary-school teacher, "It is enough to hold that the First Amendment does not entitle primary and secondary teachers, when conducting the education of captive audiences, to cover topics, or advocate viewpoints, that depart from the curriculum adopted by the school system."[13] Decisions such as that one give state legislatures ample room to suppress the discussion of divisive concepts in civics classes in public high schools. Can they do so in classes of public universities as well?

Look Who's Talking

There are cases in which it is easy to distinguish government speech from private speech. A government-run social media account, the White House press secretary, and the Secretary of State all engage in government speech. When the government buys an advertisement to encourage people to join the military or to discourage them from littering, the advertisements are government speech. When a city council adopts a resolution celebrating the achievements of the local sports team, it is engaging in government speech. When public health officials encourage individuals to get a vaccine, the exhortation is government speech. The government speaks constantly and through numerous intermediaries. It speaks on matters great and small. It sometimes conveys factual information, and it sometimes expresses value-laden messages. Sometimes the government speaks to inform, and sometimes the government speaks to persuade. When the government speaks, it gets to choose the message it wants to convey, and when the government employs an individual to communicate that message, it gets to direct the substance and form of the communication.

It is not always clear when the government is speaking, however, and that is where the Court's government speech doctrine comes in. Identifying government speech is sometimes straightforward. No one has any difficulty determining who is speaking when a roadside billboard says, "Uncle Sam wants you for the U.S. Army." In other cases, it is less clear whether a given message comes from the government or from a private actor, and it can likewise be unclear whether in a given situation an individual has a choice as to whether to communicate the government's preferred message. The Court's government speech doctrine has been concerned with teasing out the situations in which the government is speaking from those in which the private individuals are speaking. The challenge in this context is to determine whether the classroom speech of public university professors is an example of government speech, and thus can appropriately be micromanaged and directed by government officials.

The critical inquiry is, as Justice Alito has reminded us, determining "whether the government is *speaking* instead of regulating private expression."[14] I believe professorial speech is recognizably *private speech* within the frameworks the Court has provided for separating government speech from private speech. The anti-critical race theory policies are therefore best understood as efforts to regulate private expression rather than as efforts to direct government speech. Moreover, characterizing professorial speech as private speech rather than government speech is essential to realizing the aspirations of the academic freedom cases arising out of the Cold War.

Does the Government Control the Content?

The Court has not settled on a single approach to identifying government speech. Justice Breyer has characterized the Court's efforts in this regard as one of conducting "a holistic inquiry."[15] Justice Alito has characterized the Court's approach as "a fact-bound totality-of-the-circumstances inquiry."[16] In canvassing the factors that the Court has found relevant to marking out government speech, the analysis is not unambiguous but there are good reasons for thinking that professorial speech is best considered to be private expression rather than government speech.

In some recent cases, the Court has emphasized three main factors in identifying government speech: whether the history of the medium of expression "long [has] communicated messages from the government," whether the medium is "often closely identified in the public mind with the government," and whether the government maintains "direct control over the messages conveyed" through the medium.[17] These factors cut against treating professorial speech at state universities as a form of government speech.

State universities are agencies of the state and professors at those universities are government employees, but state universities have not generally been understood as vehicles for communicating messages from the government. State universities have instead generally been understood to be peculiar institutions within the state government that operate with a high degree of autonomy from state political leaders. The state maintains oversight, generally through a politically appointed board of regents, but does not attempt to direct its institutions of higher education. State officials do not specify the textbooks or detail the curriculum to be taught in universities. If state university professors were engaged in government speech when in the classroom, then we would expect government officials to comprehensively direct what it is that professors say. Instead, state officials have contented themselves with intervening only to prohibit the discussion of certain ideas in the classroom, which looks far less like using classroom lectures as vehicles for communicating messages from the government, and far more like the government censoring ideas that it does not like.

Some state constitutions enshrine an element of independence for their universities. The California Constitution of 1879, for example, specifies that the University of California "shall constitute a public trust . . . subject only to such legislative control as may be necessary to insure compliance with the terms of its endowment." The University of California was to be "entirely independent of all political or sectarian influence."[18] The launch of some state universities was accompanied by emphatic declarations of their political independence. The great education reformer James Angell began his term as president of the University of Michigan in 1871 by emphasizing that "the University cannot do its work with the highest success unless it have a certain degree of independence and self-control." The university should be "catholic and unsectarian," and the faculty should never be required to mouth "the shibboleths of sect or party."[19] Andrew Sloan Draper took the reins of the University of Illinois by declaring that public universities "must exhibit catholicity of spirit; it must tolerate all creeds; it must inspire all schools."[20] Andrew Dickson White at Cornell proclaimed, "no professor, officer, or student shall ever be accepted or rejected on account of any religious or political views which he may or may not hold."[21] State universities have historically been held out as independent institutions that were explicitly not represented to be conduits for government speech.

State universities were created to advance a public purpose but not to express a governmental message. State universities were understood to be useful for training well-educated citizens and for generating useful knowledge in the arts and sciences. Charles Van Hise at the University of Wisconsin voiced the aspiration of many in declaring, "The practical man of all practical men is he who, with his face toward truth, follows wherever it may lead." It was hoped that the unleashing of that scholarly spirit to follow the truth wherever it might lead would allow the university and its faculty "to be benefactors, not only of the state, but of the entire earth; for a new truth, a new principle, is not the property of any state, but instantly belongs to the world."[22] State universities could only accomplish their purpose if they were not restricted to repeating popular orthodoxies and if they were insulated from the expectation of being a mere mouthpiece of incumbent politicians.

There is no question that state universities are associated in the public mind with the state itself, but it seems much more dubious that the public identifies professorial speech with the state government. Indeed, a common complaint about state universities and state university professors is how divorced they are from the attitudes and perspectives of the ordinary citizens of the state. Unlike a monument on public land or a slogan emblazoned on a government ID, professorial speech is not a static message presumptively endorsed by a government. Professors are far more likely to be seen as individuals, or as part of a distinctive professorial class, than as avatars of the governments that happen to employ them. When conservatives complain about "tenured radicals" or populists complain about "pointy-headed intellectuals," they are emphasizing the gap between the professoriate and the government and community they serve.

Professorial speech is not "effectively controlled" by the government. What an individual professor might say in the classroom or in his or her scholarly research certainly is not "set out . . . from beginning to end" by the government.[23] Professorial speech is not "selected" by the government "for the purpose of presenting the image of the [government] that it wishes to project to all" who might hear it. Professors themselves are not even directly selected by "government decisionmakers" in any traditional sense but are rather selected by their faculty peers to occupy their positions.[24] Although content-based judgments are made to assess the quality of their work, they are not the kind of content-based factors that are designed to align professorial speech with governmental preferences. Scholars are chosen to advance knowledge within their discipline and not to rehearse "the shibboleths of sect or party."[25] Once professors are appointed to their positions, government officials do not "exercise editorial control" over the content of their classroom or scholarly speech.[26] To the extent that there are gatekeepers to the publication of scholarly research, it is a network of scholarly peers hailing from across the country and the globe and who likely have no connection whatsoever to the state government that might employ the author of the work. In appointing professors to the faculty of state universities, even university officials largely cede control over the content of professorial speech to the individual professor and to the larger scholarly community.

In short, professorial speech in state universities shows none of the expected characteristics of government speech. Classroom lectures in state universities have not traditionally been understood to communicate messages from the government. University professors are not associated in the public mind with the government. The government does not exercise direct control over the content of classroom lectures. This is not a situation in which "the government established the message; maintained control of its content; and controlled its dissemination to the public."[27]

Professorial speech likewise does not meet the looser analysis favored by Justice Alito for identifying government speech. The government exercises even less control over professorial speech than it does over trademark registration, for example. In a case involving a congressional ban on the government issuing trademarks that disparage individuals or groups, Justice Alito wrote for a unanimous Court in holding that trademarks are not a form of government speech but rather the speech of the entity that seeks to register the trademark. There is no examiner of professorial speech who is attempting to "inquire whether any viewpoint conveyed by [that speech] is consistent with Government policy or whether any such viewpoint is consistent with that expressed by other" professors employed at the university. Given the diversity of scholarly views of professors, if professorial speech is government speech, then the government "is babbling prodigiously and incoherently."[28] Justice

Alito's thought experiment, in a case involving specialty license plates, asked whether a reasonable observer could see myriad college football teams promoted on specialty license plates and "assume that the State of Texas was officially (and perhaps treasonously) rooting for the Longhorns' opponents?"[29] When the government creates a platform, whether a trademark or a license plate, that can be used by individuals to express a wide range of contradictory messages, it makes little sense to think that those messages are a form of government speech. And if they are not government speech, then the government cannot censor any specific messages that they do not like.

Justice Alito has identified what he considers "the minimum conditions" for identifying speech as government speech and that is that the "government purposefully expresses a message of its own through persons authorized to speak on its behalf, and in doing so, does not rely on a means that abridges private speech." "Government speech is thus the purposeful communication of a governmentally determined message by a person exercising a power to speak for a government." But no one thinks that a state university professor is "a person with the power to determine what messages the government will communicate."[30] To take but a single example, nobody believes that when Sandy Levinson, the W. St. John Garwood and W. St. John Garwood, Jr. Centennial Professor at the University of Texas School of Law, deigns to speak in class about *Marbury v. Madison*, that his views on that case are shared even by other members of the law-school faculty or the Garwood family, let alone by Governor Greg Abbott or Attorney General Ken Paxton. (Unusually among constitutional law professors, Levinson is resistant to teaching the famous case explaining the power of judicial review.)[31] Levinson is neither authorized to nor understood to be communicating "a governmentally determined message" when speaking in class at a state university. He is employed to provide his idiosyncratic scholarly expertise, not to be a spokesman for the state of Texas. His classroom speech does not "amount to government speech attributable" to the Texas government.[32]

Academic Freedom in a Government School

Recognizing that a professor's speech in a classroom "represent[s] his own private speech"[33] and not government speech is ultimately necessary to preserving the logic and goals of the Court's academic freedom jurisprudence. The stated purpose of protecting academic freedom under the First Amendment is to prevent "laws that cast a pall of orthodoxy over the classroom."[34] If classroom speech is best understood as government speech, then the entire point would be to impose orthodoxy. Students might not have to accept that orthodoxy as true, but professors would be obliged to convey it. If professors are paid strictly to toe the company line when speaking to students, it would have "an unmistakable tendency to chill that free play of the spirit which all teachers ought especially to cultivate and practice."[35]

The academic freedom cases defend the possibility that professors in their classrooms will dissent from the government's own policies, principles, and values. Indeed, at the heart of the academic freedom cases was whether professors could advocate that the United States government itself be dissolved. There is no sense in which Paul Sweezy's lecture to the students in a class at the University of New Hampshire could be regarded as government speech. For the Court to uphold the right of Sweezy and others like him to teach the truth as he understood it in state university classrooms, that speech had to be understood as private speech subject to First Amendment protection. And it had to be understood as private speech subject to First Amendment protection, even when expressed by a state university professor acting pursuant to his official duties as an instructor in a classroom.

That is not to say that there may be no government speech on state university campuses. The government might require, for example, that an official governmental statement be included in course syllabi or distributed to university students, comparable to the "ministerial" speech that university officials sometimes require of faculty.[36] It is not obvious that ministerial speech must also be "non-ideological" in order to be consistent with First Amendment protections for academic freedom. A professor cannot be compelled to endorse ideological statements or express them as her own without running afoul of the protections outlined in the Flag Salute Case. But if, for example, a state university required a professor to convey the state's own ideologically freighted message in a manner that made clear that the message came from the state and not from the professor, then it is not apparent that the professor's First Amendment rights have been infringed. Even if it is permissible for a university to require a professor to include the government's message in the form of a specified land acknowledgment or diversity statement in a course syllabus, it is surely not permissible for a university to compel a professor to present such a message as if it were the professor's own or to refrain from supplementing the government's message with an alternative viewpoint on that topic.[37]

The government might specially authorize particular programming or even particular classes and course materials in which professors might choose to participate. In that way, government officials might supplement the regular academic offerings of the university and exercise greater editorial control over that specific subset of academic activities in a manner that made it clear that the course content was in fact government speech. In short, the government might, consistent with academic freedom, *add* government speech to the intellectual life of a state university, so long as it does so in a manner that does not restrain or crowd out the freedom of members of the faculty to express countervailing ideas in the course of their teaching and scholarship. It cannot, however, displace private professorial speech with government speech or use government speech as a cover for censoring private professorial speech. To borrow from a different line of First Amendment doctrine, in adding government speech to a university environment, the state must "leave open ample alternative channels" for communicating the private professorial speech protected by academic freedom.[38]

The government might even transform the nature of state universities so that they are truly government schools in the most robust sense. If a state were to resolve to comprehensively direct the university curriculum as it does the primary and secondary school curriculum, it would mark a revolutionary transformation in public higher education in the United States. And it might also signal the end of academic freedom in those schools. No state has sought to treat higher education as it does secondary education, or to say of a university board of trustees what can be said of a local school board, that "[o]nly the school board has ultimate responsibility for what goes on in the classroom, legitimately giving it a say over what teachers may (or may not) teach in the classroom."[39] Whether the First Amendment creates an impassable obstacle to a state attempting to exercise such control over a university is a distinguishable question from whether a state can attempt to impose discrete constraints on professorial speech given the kinds of universities that they have established.[40]

The notion of a state converting its state universities into glorified high schools is perhaps not as far-fetched as it seems at first. There is a bright line between a student's last day in high school and first day in college, but that line is somewhat arbitrary and has gotten dimmer. The state closely regulates the curriculum and its content throughout the secondary school, and it employs and supervises teachers of twelfth-grade students in the same manner that it employs and supervises teachers of sixth-grade students. But who is to say that the first year of postsecondary school could not instead be organized as the thirteenth year of primary and secondary school? The gap between the two has already been blurred by the heavy use of an Advanced Placement curriculum adopted wholesale from an outside vendor and advertised as providing "college-level work" for "college credit and placement." Other secondary schools have established dual enrollment programs that allow high-school students to take college classes while attending high school. Part of the logic of using two-year associate degrees as a steppingstone to a four-year bachelor's degree is that the entry-level classes in most colleges are more of a commodity than a differentiated product. It is not a new observation that the general education of the first two years of college in form and purpose are comparable to the upper grades of high school. It is not until students reach the final years of their study that they begin to specialize, to tread closer to the frontiers of knowledge, and to develop the habits of mind that characterize a true scholar. It is on that frontier that students and teachers both need the most freedom to explore new ideas and exercise independent judgment.

Could states reconstitute their postsecondary education with a system of distinct junior and senior colleges, with the latter doing the characteristic work of higher education but the former focusing on the transmission of information? Could junior colleges be subjected to the same type of close political oversight that characterizes secondary education, such that they are well understood to be in the business of delivering a state-approved curriculum and attempting to instill state-preferred values? The change would be dramatic, but not out of the question. An instructor accepting a job in such a public junior college might expect to have no more academic freedom than a teacher in a public high school. Public officials, not instructors, would choose both the content of the class and the viewpoint to be expressed regarding that content. It seems implausible that the First Amendment could be an absolute bar to such a reform of postsecondary education. But that is not the kind of public postsecondary schools that we have now. Given the choices the state has thus far made about how it wants to organize higher education, the First Amendment becomes relevant.

Could the state go even further and reduce all elements of a university to such a politically regimented model? Certainly, no university organized in such a fashion would be regarded as a serious institution of higher learning. Such an approach would drain the public university of all of its intellectual vitality. Whether the First Amendment would prohibit a state from embarking on such an experiment seems doubtful. Academic freedom is a contingent fact of the kinds of universities that currently exist in the United States. At one time, private universities denied academic freedom to their faculties, and trustees exercised unquestioned authority over what ideas could be discussed or professed within their domain. Public universities could resurrect that model, with politically elected or appointed boards of governors dictating to professors what and how they could teach. The same logic that courts have applied to primary and secondary schools could be applied by them to postsecondary schools as well. "The Constitution does not prohibit a State from creating elected school boards and from placing responsibility for the curriculum of each school district in the hands of each board."

Perhaps there are salient differences between the secondary and postsecondary schools, differences that would prevent such a move. Courts have found it relevant, for example, that students are required to attend secondary schools, that they are minors, and that their parents retain authority over the direction of their education. "Parents long have demanded that school boards control the curriculum and the ways of teaching it to their impressionable children," and the First Amendment cannot be read to give individual teachers a right to "introduce mature sexual themes to fifteen-year-olds" or assign to children "materials that members of the community perceive as racially insensitive."[41] But students are not compelled by the state to sit in a college professor's class, and college students are not minor children under the authority of their parents. Even so, perhaps the state could create "a proprietary school or college designed for the propagation of specific doctrines by those who have furnished its endowment," in this case the elected representatives of the people of the state.[42] If students chose to attend such an institution and professors chose to be employed by it, then *caveat emptor*.

Identifying such possible limits on the scope of First Amendment protection for public university professors can wait until another day. No state has constituted its institutions of higher education on such a foundation. No state has taken the steps that would be necessary to transform public universities into instruments of government speech. Ad hoc legislative gags on what professors may say so that they may be prevented from expressing ideas that displease politicians or the electoral majority are clearly different. They do not direct government speech so that the government can get its own favored ideas into the intellectual marketplace. They censor private speech so as to remove some ideas from the marketplace and to try to constrict what ideas citizens can think.

7

Compelling Students to Believe

The dominant strategy of state government officials who wish to suppress disfavored ideas from being taught on university campuses has been to prohibit the advocacy, advancement, or promotion of those ideas in the classroom. Such proposals run into the constitutional problems examined in the last two chapters – to what degree can state governments bar professors from promoting disfavored ideas in public university classrooms. I believe the First Amendment obstacles to such an effort to gag state university faculty are formidable. If there is any meaningful constitutional protection for academic freedom, it should pose a barrier to politicians picking and choosing which viewpoints may or may not be advanced in a public university classroom.

A second strategy is more subtle, and the constitutional issues it raises are even more complex. It is also more modest in its effects and, as a result, is less likely to be satisfactory to those who would wish to see "divisive concepts" rooted out of American universities. Much of its effect would likely come from the chilling effect it would produce as professors sought to steer a clear path around any legislative prohibitions.

This second strategy focuses on professorial speech that seeks to "inculcate" or "compel" students to believe in specified disfavored ideas. This too derives from President Donald Trump's executive order barring divisive concepts in federal workplace training. The executive order prohibited training that "teaches, advocates, or promotes ... divisive concepts," but it also directed that federal agencies "shall not use any workplace training that inculcates in its employees" those specified divisive concepts.[1] Florida's Stop WOKE Act combined these elements into a single prohibition on subjecting "any student or employee to training or instruction that espouses, promotes, advances, inculcates, or compels such student or employee to believe" any of a list of specified divisive concepts.[2] A bill that passed the Texas state senate but failed in the Texas state house reflects a further evolution of such policies. Texas Senate Bill 16 directed that "a faculty member of an institution of higher education may not compel or attempt to compel a student enrolled at the institution to adopt a belief that any race, sex, or ethnicity or social, political, or religious belief is inherently superior to any other race, sex, ethnicity, or belief." If a university determined that a faculty member had violated that statutory provision, the professor was to be fired.[3] If the initial wave of divisive concepts legislation took aim at professors who "promote" politically disfavored ideas in the classroom, a second wave of legislation is likely to target members of the faculty who are alleged to have compelled students to believe in such ideas.

It is notable that a federal district judge's opinion enjoining implementation of the Stop WOKE Act chose to use the shorthand of "promote or compel" in referring to the prohibited speech, even though the court recognized that the various terms were not "synonymous (or even similar)."[4] In fact, the court was only concerned with faculty speech that might promote such beliefs, in part because the professors who brought the suit denied that they had any intention of compelling any specific belief. Such a shorthand will not do, as states consider policies that look more like the one that was nearly adopted by the Texas state legislature in 2023, and the constitutional issues with bills like Texas S.B. 16 are quite distinct. In time, courts will have to confront the constitutional issues associated with laws that simply prohibit members of the faculty compelling belief.

The focus of this chapter is on the constitutional issues raised by policies prohibiting state university professors from attempting to compel a student's belief in any particular idea.[5] Such language of compelling belief in fact borrows from constitutional doctrine. The Court has made clear that the state, and its employees, may not compel beliefs. As a result, on the face of it, a policy like that advanced in Texas S.B. 16 only prohibits acts that would already be a violation of a student's constitutional rights under the First Amendment. It would be naive to think that such policies would do no work at all and are designed to do nothing more than restate the status quo. It is worth thinking through what such policies would be doing, and what, if any, problems they present.

This chapter identifies what kind of faculty behavior might run afoul of such statutory prohibitions and what concerns the laws might raise for academic freedom. What might be entailed by compelling belief in ideas is much less clear than what is entailed by promoting beliefs, and so it is necessary to examine carefully how courts have thought about compelled belief under the terms of the First Amendment and what that might imply about these policies. The First Amendment is already understood to bar government officials, including public university professors, from compelling belief, and so there are already some guidelines in place that can guide courts and university officials as they attempt to implement such a ban. There is some conduct that professors would be wise to avoid so as not to run afoul of such bans. But these legislative bans do not simply mirror the constitutional prohibition on compelled belief, and so they both create a risk of improper administrative interference with faculty teaching and invite the possibility of courts striking them down as raising constitutional problems of their own.

The Flag Salute Case

We have had occasion to mention the Flag Salute Case before. The Flag Salute Case has particular historical significance in establishing that, as the Court later put it, neither "students nor teachers shed their constitutional rights to freedom of speech or expression at the schoolhouse gate."[6] Justice Robert Jackson's soaring rhetoric in the majority opinion in decrying the government imposition of orthodoxies has resonated across numerous First Amendment cases, including those concerned with academic freedom.

The case stands for a more specific constitutional proposition, that the state may not compel speech or belief. The compelled speech doctrine is one of the foundational features of American free-speech jurisprudence, but it is also one that remains mired in opacity. Even though the compelled speech doctrine arose in the context of education, what compelled speech might mean in a classroom context is especially unclear. The Court has yet to provide much guidance for the perplexed.

This does not bode well for a legislative effort to protect a student's right to be free from compelled speech. If a state were to do no more than provide a legal redress in cases in which a student's right against compelled speech has been violated, the courts would be challenged to separate out the cases in which the right had been violated from those in which it had not. We know that there is a right against compelled speech, but judges might be reluctant to say that they even know it when they see it, let alone that they could articulate a clear rule that could guide others seeking to avoid the prohibited acts.

In fact, states adopting such laws are doing more than merely providing a remedy for known rights violations. They are directing universities to create a system of surveillance to monitor the classroom speech of professors in order to detect politically objectionable speech and punish professors for engaging in it. Moreover, they are drawing a line that the Constitution itself does not. These policies are not designed to protect students from compelled belief. They are designed to protect students from being compelled to believe ideas that politicians do not like. The Constitution does not allow politicians to play such favorites.

But let us start at the beginning.

Laws requiring that public schoolchildren salute the American flag and say the Pledge of Allegiance were a product of the First World War. The patriotic fervor that put pressure on academic freedom at the start of the war continued to have ripple effects after the war was over. Newly created veteran groups like the American Legion lobbied for patriotic exercises in the schools and promoted the public display of the American flag. By the start of the Second World War, several states had adopted laws requiring a flag salute exercise in public schools and such exercises were common across the country. In the midst of the war, Congress for the first time wrote into federal law the American Legion's flag code and the Pledge of Allegiance, though the federal statute included no legal mandates.

Not everyone was enthusiastic about the new patriotic exercises. In particular, the Jehovah's Witnesses decided that the flag salute contradicted their religious beliefs. The Witnesses are a Christian religious sect started in Pennsylvania not long after the Civil War. Among the church's distinctive teachings was the expectation of the imminent arrival of the Apocalypse, and its members soon became known for their particularly aggressive brand of proselytizing. Impressed by the example of their German followers who refused to give the "Hitler salute,"

Joseph Rutherford, then the leader of the church, praised their example at a church convention in Washington, D.C. in 1935 and urged his American followers to do the same. Rutherford denounced the "flag-saluting cult" for its "deification of the flag" and encouragement of a form of idolatry. In Hitler's Germany, the cost of adhering to these religious scruples was for many death in a concentration camp. In the United States, it sometimes resulted in expulsion from the public school, as well as more severe mob justice.[7]

Such was the case for a group of children in Minersville, Pennsylvania. Unlike others, Walter Gobitas sued on behalf of his children, carrying the dispute all the way to the U.S. Supreme Court. In an opinion written by Felix Frankfurter, the Court overwhelmingly favored the school, holding that religious conscience did not relieve "the individual from obedience to a general law not aimed at the promotion or restriction of religious beliefs." Sincerely held religious beliefs could not trump the requirements of a general law that served a legitimate, secular purpose. Frankfurter thought that courts should not insist that an "exceptional immunity must be given to dissidents." A "free people" should fight out the wisdom of such accommodations "in the forum of public opinion and before legislative assemblies" and not depend on judges to make the necessary trade-offs.[8]

In a lone dissent, Justice Harlan F. Stone sketched out a very different vision of how the courts should approach cases involving civil liberties and of the issue at stake in the case. In cases "where there are competing demands of the interests of government and of liberty under the Constitution . . . it is the function of courts to determine whether such an accommodation is reasonably possible." The existence of "specific constitutional restrictions" necessitated taking those judgments out of the hands of the forum of public opinion and legislative assemblies. More concretely, Stone thought the flag-salute requirement "is unique in the history of Anglo-American legislation" in seeking "to coerce these children to express a sentiment which, as they interpret it, they do not entertain, and which violates their deepest religious convictions." Stone thought the "very essence of the liberty" secured by the First Amendment "is the freedom of the individual from compulsion as to what he shall think and what he shall say, at least where the compulsion is to bear false witness to his religion." Stone, like Frankfurter, still thought of this as primarily a religious freedom case, but it cut close to the core of constitutional protection of religious conscience by attempting "to secure conformity of belief and opinion by a compulsory affirmation of the desired belief."[9]

Surprisingly, the Court was soon ready to reverse itself. In private, Frankfurter confessed to Stone that the case weighed on him, but he thought it cost dissidents little simply to make "a gesture of respect for the symbol of our national being" and resolved to make the case into "a vehicle for preaching the true democratic faith of not relying on the Court for the impossible task of assuring vigorous, mature, self-protecting and tolerant democracy."[10] The Court's decision in *Gobitis* might have been popular in the countryside, but elite opinion ran strongly in favor of Stone's dissent. Liberal intellectuals were shocked by their friend Frankfurter's willingness to subordinate his own civil libertarian credentials to the "true democratic faith," though the justice proved immune to their criticism. The growing spate of violence directed at the Witnesses spurred a backlash, at least among leading lawyers. Solicitor General Francis Biddle delivered a nationally broadcast speech warning, "We shall not defeat the Nazi evil by emulating its methods."[11] Three members of the *Gobitis* majority soon announced that they had changed their minds on the need for "our democratic form of government . . . to accommodate itself to the religious views of minorities, however unpopular and unorthodox those views may be," and two others left the bench.[12] Justice Stone had since been promoted to chief justice.

The vehicle for a reconsideration of *Gobitis* arrived in the form of *West Virginia State Board of Education v. Barnette*, which the Court decided in 1943. The state board of education quoted from the *Gobitis* opinion in adopting a requirement that schoolchildren salute the flag. Witness children continued to defy those requirements, and Harry Covington, the legal counsel for the Watch Tower Bible and Tract Society, found some West Virginia families willing to be parties to the suit.

Frankfurter now found himself writing for only three justices in dissent. Frankfurter continued to see the controversy as primarily one of a religious minority demanding a judicially created exception to a generally applicable statute. While he professed himself personally in agreement with the "general libertarian views" expressed by the Court's new majority, he refused to write "my private notions of policy into the Constitution."[13]

Newly appointed Justice Robert H. Jackson wrote for the majority of six justices. As U.S. Attorney General, Jackson had led a Justice Department that had been investigating the persecution of the Witnesses during the Second World War. Jackson was not always sympathetic to the Witnesses, whom the free-speech pioneer Zechariah Chafee described as having "astonishing powers of annoyance."[14] In this context, however, he was clearly moved by their mistreatment. His initial draft of the majority opinion was sprinkled with references to the violence directed at the sect during the war before Stone persuaded him to take them out so as not to imply that the Court could be swayed by such extralegal considerations.[15]

Although there are echoes of Stone's *Gobitis* dissent in the *Barnette* opinion, Jackson dramatically reconceptualized the framing of the case. In his hands the flag salute laws were no longer about religious conscience at all. This was now a free-speech case. The new framing allowed him to sidestep entirely the knotty problem of religious exemptions from legal obligations. The dissident schoolchildren stood not on the superiority of their religious faith but "on a right of self-determination in matters that touch individual opinion and personal attitude."[16]

At stake in the flag salute controversy, Jackson thought, was whether a democratic state could compel its citizens to express loyalty to a political belief. The students in West Virginia were "not merely made acquainted with the flag salute so that they may be informed as to what it is or even what it means." They were compelled "to declare a belief." He compared it to requirements in ancient Rome that Christians must "participate in ceremonies before the statue of the emperor or other symbol of imperial authority." The state was requiring "the individual to communicate by word and sign his acceptance of the political ideas" represented by the flag. The mandatory salute "requires affirmation of a belief and an attitude of mind," whether the students must become "unwilling converts" or must only engage in a simulation of "assent by words without belief."[17]

The right of free speech would be imperfect, Jackson argued, if it "guards the individual's right to speak his own mind," but "left it open to public authorities to compel him to utter what is not in his mind." If the state could compel this particular pledge of loyalty, it could likewise "force an American citizen publicly to profess any statement of belief" it might wish. The American experiment rested on the strength of the "individual freedom of mind" rather than that of "officially disciplined uniformity." Public education must "not be partisan or enemy of any class, creed, party, or faction," nor may it seek "to impose any ideological discipline" on its students. It may not "coerce uniformity of sentiment" but could only attempt to persuade. "Authority here is to be controlled by public opinion, not public opinion by authority." No government official in America "can prescribe what shall be orthodox in politics, nationalism, religion, or other matters of opinion or force citizens to confess by word of act their faith therein."[18]

Compelling Speech in School

A right against compelled speech is an appealing idea, but what does it actually mean? The courts have struggled to identify a coherent principle in *Barnette* that can readily be applied in other contexts. The easiest cases have turned out to be situations in which individuals are involuntarily drafted into becoming the government's messenger. The government is free to speak and express the specific messages it desires, but it is not free to compel others to deliver those messages on its behalf. Similarly, all members of our society have the freedom to speak their own mind, but they do not have the freedom to force others to speak those ideas as well. Thus, the Court has been skeptical of government programs that force individuals to provide resources for speech to which they object.[19] Individual citizens cannot be forced to become billboards for government speech.[20] Additionally, the government cannot water down or obscure a citizen's own speech by forcing that individual to simultaneously mouth the government's preferred speech.[21]

A constitutional prohibition on compelled speech is particularly daunting to implement in the context of education. The compelled speech doctrine has been boiled down to a simple "principle that freedom of speech prohibits the government from telling people what they must say."[22] But a central feature of the educational context is that teachers tell students what they must say all the time. Students are told to recite poems and translate passages. They are told to summarize what an author has said or read aloud passages from a text. They are told to write an essay arguing for a particular thesis and they are told to accurately explain a scientific theory. Compelled speech is pervasive in schools, including those that are run by the government and bound by the First Amendment. If an instructor could not compel speech from a student, much of the standard educational process would be thrown into disarray.

The U.S. Supreme Court has asserted that at "the heart of the First Amendment lies the principle that each person should decide for himself or herself the ideas and beliefs deserving of expression, consideration, and adherence" but, as a federal circuit court later observed, "this particular right is necessarily different in the public school setting." The "educational process itself may sometimes require a state actor to force a student to speak when the student would rather refrain. A student may also be forced to speak or write on a particular topic even though the student might prefer a different topic."[23] "A teacher may require a student to write a paper from a particular viewpoint, even if it is a viewpoint with which the student disagrees." "A law-school professor may assign students to write 'opinions' showing how Justices Ginsburg and Scalia would analyze a particular Fourth Amendment question."[24] Students may be compelled by the threat of a bad grade to speak when they would prefer to remain silent and to express specified ideas, even when they would prefer to express different ideas or believe the ideas that they are forced to express are wrong.

The Court did not mean to outlaw education in *Barnette*, so how can we distinguish the impermissible compelled speech in West Virginia's patriotic exercise from the permissible compelled speech that took place throughout the rest of the school day? Of course, one easy but not very helpful answer is that the requirement in *Barnette* was *sui generis*. If an instructor were to attempt to compel a student to salute the flag and pledge allegiance to the republic for which it stands, he would be violating the student's rights as stated in *Barnette*. And, perhaps only the most closely analogous situations would also be covered by the rule. If so, state legislation prohibiting professors from compelling beliefs would be of little practical consequence.

But even when confronted with very similar cases, courts have found *Barnette* inadequate. A student who refused to stand while the pledge was being recited was exercising her

constitutional rights, but the right she was exercising was less
one of refusing to engage in compelled speech (the New Jersey
statute in that case allowed students to abstain from reciting
the pledge) than one of engaging in an act of symbolic expression by remaining seated.[25] A student who stood silently with
a raised fist while the class recited the pledge needed not only
a right to refuse to say the pledge but also the right to make
the symbolic protest of the raised fist.[26] A federal circuit court
concluded that a student did not have a constitutional right to
refuse to participate in an assignment to salute the Mexican
flag and recite the Mexican Pledge of Allegiance in a Spanish
class, but the same circuit also thought it was at least possible
that a sociology teacher's assignment that students transcribe
the American Pledge of Allegiance violated their right against
compelled speech.[27]

The courts have largely come to settle on a principle that
distinguishes between permissible and impermissible compelled speech in schools, but the result is that in practice
very little compelled speech in school is impermissible. It is
constitutionally permissible for instructors to compel speech
from students when the speech is "related to learning."[28] The
Supreme Court held in 1988 that school officials could exercise
"editorial control over the style and content of student speech
in school-expressive activities so long as their actions are
reasonably related to legitimate pedagogical concerns."[29] That
case involved a high-school principal in Hazelwood School
District removing two articles from the student newspaper,
and so was not directly concerned with compelled speech at
all. Nonetheless, lower courts have concluded that censoring
student speech was simply the flip side of compelling student
speech, and that "school-expressive activities" could readily be
extended from extracurricular activities, like a school newspaper, to curricular activities, like a classroom assignment, and
so the rule announced in *Hazelwood* established a general rule
for understanding how to reconcile student speech rights with

the authority of schools to advance their educational mission. Moreover, for this purpose, courts have accepted that the rule works just as well for public universities as for public secondary schools. The critical question for determining whether a particular instance of compelled speech in a school is constitutionally permissible is whether it is "reasonably related to legitimate pedagogical concerns." If the compelled speech is intended to serve an educational purpose, it is constitutionally permissible.

What does this leave out, other than the flag salute situation itself? Since school officials are unlikely to explicitly attempt to compel speech without an educational purpose, the most relevant possibility is when a school official acts pretextually. That is, a teacher might purport to have an educational purpose that justifies attempting to compel speech, but that stated purpose might simply be a pretense. Such pretextual actions might mirror legitimate educational activities, but the context in which they occur indicates that they do not in fact serve any legitimate educational purpose. Imagine, for example, that a devout Muslim is teaching a class on world history and a devout Jew is a student in the class, and the instructor and student find themselves in heated disagreements about Islamic history and countries. The instructor then directs the student to write "Allahu Akbar" one thousand times on the chalkboard in the classroom. There are myriad circumstances in which a teacher directing a student to repeatedly write a message on a chalkboard would serve a legitimate educational purpose. The context in which this particular instruction was made to the student, however, would suggest that the educational rationale is pretextual and the compelled speech is impermissible. Imagine a case in which a modest woman in a literature class makes clear that she is uncomfortable with coarse language and sexual references. The instructor then begins to call on that student to read aloud passages from the assigned texts when those passages contain precisely such content. There are many occasions when asking a student to read aloud from a text in a class would serve a valid educational purpose but, again, the circumstances in this case would suggest that the educational purpose is a pretext and the instructor is simply singling out this student to harass her and make her uncomfortable. The inquiry in such cases is not whether this example of compelled classroom speech is the kind of thing that is educationally appropriate, but whether this particular instance of compelled speech actually serves a legitimate educational purpose.

Such inquiries are not necessarily easy, but the principled distinction between using the classroom to instruct and using the classroom for other purposes is of critical importance. Academic freedom protects the former, but not the latter. A federal circuit court aptly summarized the issue as it has appeared in lawsuits over how teachers have conducted themselves in the classroom: "So long as the teacher limits speech or grades speech in the classroom in the name of learning and not as a pretext for punishing the student for her race, gender, economic class, religion, or political persuasion, the federal courts should not interfere." A teacher who failed a student for writing an essay on an unapproved topic was using her available tools of state coercion to compel the student to write something that the student preferred not to write, but "it is the essence of the teacher's responsibility in the classroom to draw lines and make distinctions – in a word to encourage speech germane to the topic at hand and discourage speech unlikely to shed light on the subject."[30] Professors who single out "one student for discipline based on hostility to her speech" will have a difficult time justifying their actions, but "the neutral enforcement of a legitimate school curriculum generally will satisfy" the requirement that restrictions on student speech or compelled student speech are related to legitimate pedagogical concerns.[31] Professors "routinely require students to express a viewpoint that is not their own in order to teach students to think critically," and thus "requiring an acting student, in the context of a classroom exercise, to speak the words of a script as written is no different from requiring that a law or history student argue a position with which he disagrees." Courts should only "override an educator's judgment where the proffered goal or methodology was a sham pretext for an impermissible ulterior motive."[32]

Instructors might be misguided and give assignments to students that are ineffective or otherwise are inadvisable given their educational goals, but such assignments would not therefore be constitutionally impermissible. Instructors may make mistakes without violating their students' First Amendment rights. But, if it is implausible that a particular assignment is intended to serve an educational goal, then the instructor has not merely failed to perform his job well. He has engaged in punishable misconduct. Such misconduct would fall outside the bounds of traditional academic freedom protections. In the context of a state university, it could also create legal liability for a rights violation. Both private and public universities would have a valid interest in identifying such classroom misconduct and putting a stop to it. Instructors need the ability to compel their students to express particular messages in order to perform their educational duties, but they have no right or justification to impose such compulsions if they are not related to learning.

In sum, state university professors do not have the freedom to use their authority in the classroom for purposes unrelated to the education of their students. In fact, professors would be violating the First Amendment rights of their students were they to force those students to express ideas without a legitimate educational purpose. University officials already have a legal obligation to address such professional misconduct. Educators are in the unusual position of having the authority to compel students to express ideas with which the student disagrees or would prefer not to express, but they must take care not to abuse that authority. The proposed policies are not merely concerned with such abuses, however. Those policies purport not to ban compelled speech in the university classroom, but to ban compelled belief. What might be the difference?

Compelling Belief in School

The *Barnette* decision has come to stand for a constitutional right not to have to engage in compelled speech. The government generally cannot make individuals say things that they do not want to say, though there are exceptions, and among them is an exception for students involved in a legitimate educational activity.

But *Barnette* most directly advanced a somewhat different and narrower proposition, that individuals have a constitutional right not to be *compelled to adopt a belief* in particular ideas. Identifying cases in which individuals are compelled to believe something is even more difficult than identifying cases in which individuals are improperly compelled to speak. A constitutional shield against compelled beliefs, however, might best capture why the Court thought West Virginia's flag salute mandate was different from and worse than the myriad other mandates to which West Virginia children were subjected over the course of the school day. Teasing out the characteristics of an attempt to compel belief is a subtle exercise, so subtle in fact that it might help explain why courts have struggled to identify situations that are closely analogous to the requirement that the Court struck down in *Barnette*.

What exactly is it about the flag salute mandate that made it so constitutionally problematic? *Hazelwood* might not be an adequate explanation. *Hazelwood* tells us that compelled speech in an educational context that does not serve a legitimate educational purpose is impermissible. But why should we say that a flag salute mandate does not serve a legitimate educational purpose? If a state wants, as West Virginia did, to teach, foster, and perpetuate "the ideals, principles and spirit of Americanism," requiring teachers to lead students in a salute to the American flag might well be a means to that end. It might not be an especially effective means to that end, but it is not obvious why a daily or weekly salute to the flag is not "related to learning" or fails to have a "pedagogical purpose." A flag salute exercise is not a "sham pretext for an impermissible ulterior motive." If the state can permissibly attempt to foster the spirit of Americanism in the students attending its schools, saluting the flag could rationally be included in that curriculum. Indeed, the veterans in the American Legion likely thought that promulgating their flag code would be beneficial to fostering patriotism because they themselves had been taught to revere the flag during their military service through exactly those kinds of compelled rituals.

Perhaps the key here is less about whether the flag salute serves an educational purpose than whether it serves a *legitimate* educational purpose. If so, it is not because fostering patriotism is an illegitimate educational purpose. The courts have firmly acknowledged that American public schools can permissibly seek to instill community values in their students. The Court has observed that "the public educator nurtures students' social and moral development by transmitting to them an official dogma of 'community values.'"[33] An important function of public schools is "the preparation of individuals for participation as citizens, and in the preservation of the values on which society rests." Schools quite properly set about the task of "inculcating fundamental values necessary to the maintenance of a democratic political system."[34] It is precisely for this reason that "patriotic" "viewpoints will be expressed in the classroom" that public schools and their curricula are ultimately accountable to "someone the people can vote out of office, rather than tenured teachers."[35] This may be particularly true of primary and secondary schools, but it is true to some degree of postsecondary schools as well. If the flag salute does not serve a *legitimate* pedagogical purpose, the problem must be the means rather than the end the state was seeking to achieve.

This brings us back to what Justice Jackson thought was distinctive about the flag salute mandate – that it attempted to compel belief. The state was not just informing students about the flag and what it means, it was attempting "a compulsion of students to declare a belief." The state was not satisfied with the "slow and easily neglected route to aroused loyalties" through argument and persuasion. It was looking for a "shortcut by substituting a compulsory salute and slogan." The result was "rather pathetic" in its neglect of any serious engagement with students to lead them to understand the principles of the republic or the history of the country. West Virginia "contemplates that students forego any contrary convictions of their own" and "communicate by word and sign [their] acceptance of the political ideas" embodied in the Pledge of Allegiance. The state claimed the authority not only to compel speech, but also "to coerce acceptance" of a patriotic creed. Americans could not, Jackson thought, be forced "publicly to profess any statement of belief or to engage in any ceremony of assent to one." The "individual freedom of mind" was at stake in such state efforts to compel belief, and it was this political effort to "coerce uniformity of sentiment" that was most objectionable about what the West Virginia Board of Education had done.[36]

These potential signs of attempts to coerce belief have likewise been important markers for the lower courts, when seeking to ferret out impermissible acts by school officials. "The constitutional line is crossed when, instead of merely teaching, the educators demand that students express agreement with the educators' values." If "students are obliged to adopt an organization's objectionable philosophy" as part of the school curriculum, then serious constitutional issues would arise. But if students are merely being asked to learn about and work with ideas and organizations that they find objectionable and

are not "obliged to express their belief, either orally or in writing," in that which they find disagreeable, then no serious First
Amendment issues arise. State schools can "point students
toward values generally shared by the community," but the
state may not confine students "to the expression of those sen-
timents that are officially approved."[37]

Students must be allowed to disagree with the ideas promoted by their instructors. When the circuit court examined
the case of a sociology teacher requiring students to transcribe the Pledge of Allegiance, it thought there was nothing
objectionable about the assignment as such. The question that
needed to be answered was whether the teacher was forcing the
students "to swear allegiance" or "swear their fealty and devotion" by the act of writing out the Pledge. When a dissenting
judge worried that the court was opening the door to federal
lawsuits whenever students were required to "memorize and
write down" passages from a controversial text, the response
was that the fault, if there was one, was not the memorization
or recitation but in the swearing of fealty. A teacher was free
to require engagement with a set of ideas, and even to hope "to
foster respect" for those ideas, but a teacher would be crossing a line if she insisted on an expression of affirmation and
belief.[38] This is what the court thought distinguished the case
of the Spanish teacher requiring students to recite the Mexican
Pledge of Allegiance from the situation in *Barnette*. The ceremony in *Barnette* "was not just a tool to shape learning. It
was also a tool to compel patriotism, and this latter goal was
unacceptable." If the evidence suggested that the recitation
of a pledge was "part of a cultural and educational exercise,"
then that was one thing. If it was instead "trying to motivate
the students to become loyal to Mexico" or had as its purpose
a desire "to compel the speaker's affirmative belief," then that
was quite another. A classroom exercise that "was seeking to
force orthodoxy" was constitutionally distinguishable from a
classroom exercise that "may compel some speech."[39]

Even if the mandatory flag salute served some educational purpose, it would be constitutionally impermissible. It is impermissible not simply because it compels a student to engage in speech that the student might not believe or want to say. It is impermissible because it seeks to secure patriotism and fealty through compulsion rather than through persuasion. It seeks to enforce orthodoxy by excluding the possibility of critique or dissent. It demands that students adopt as their own beliefs that they do not share. It attempts to root out freedom of thought by forcing a student to affirm that he has adopted the required attitude of mind. It tells the student that she must "modify her values" or suffer penalties from agents of the state.[40] Such demands from the government are inappropriate in a political system founded on the consent of the governed, and the First Amendment reflects and secures that fundamental commitment to self-government.

What Could a Ban on Compelling Belief Do?

This brings us back to these proposed legislative interventions into classroom teaching. A running theme of these proposals is to prohibit attempts by state university professors to compel the adoption of politically disfavored beliefs by their students. These measures have rarely been explained by their advocates, and they have largely avoided examination from their critics. The threat to ban the promotion of disfavored ideas is seemingly more immediate and consequential. Moreover, professors readily imagine themselves advancing or promoting ideas in their classrooms, but they do not imagine themselves compelling beliefs. It is tempting to think that a ban on compelled beliefs is therefore inconsequential.

That would likely be a mistake. How courts might interpret such measures is far from clear, but it would seem likely that they would be driven back to *Barnette* as the source of such language and quite possibly trace the path outlined in this chapter. Meanwhile university administrators, urged on by politicians and activists, will be tempted to adopt an even broader interpretation of these prohibitions. When students complain that they are being "indoctrinated" or "gagged" by their professors, they are likely to find some sympathetic ears and such policies will give them a ready weapon to be used against disliked members of the faculty. Legislation is rarely treated as an empty gesture. Conduct would be found that is seen as running afoul of such bans. Professors would have to learn how to give such policies a wide berth and self-censor, so as to avoid stumbling into some legal pitfall. A prohibition on attempts to compel disfavored beliefs will not cut as wide a swath through the educational landscape as a prohibition on espousing disfavored ideas, but it would have consequences.

As we have seen, one tactic that courts have adopted to identify impermissible efforts to compel speech is to search for pretexts hiding ulterior motives. Such a pretext is most readily revealed when a student is singled out for different treatment. Such misconduct is already unlawful in a state institution. A professor who singled a student out for differential treatment invites questions as to whether the professor is encroaching on the student's constitutional rights. If new legislation adds teeth to that constitutional prohibition, university officials will be encouraged to take complaints of differential treatment quite seriously.

A statutory ban on attempts to compel beliefs might also force an investigator to shift the search for ulterior motives from the treatment of individuals to the treatment of groups. There can no longer be a default assumption that the normal treatment of students serves a proper educational purpose, such that the departures from those norms are likely to be improper. Instead, a statutory ban would encourage a more searching scrutiny of the normal and routine conduct of instructors. It might serve to shift the burden of proof. Rather than simply assuming that the routine is proper and permissible, it will drive university administrators to ask more skeptical questions about how exactly a particular classroom practice actually advances a legitimate pedagogical purpose. Students who are unhappy with what they are made to say in the classroom will have a new tool for raising objections to such requirements and demanding a sufficiently satisfying explanation of the educational value of the instructor's conduct and methods.

Courts have traditionally adopted a deferential posture when it comes to scrutinizing the classroom activity of instructors on the theory that teachers exercise a wide range of discretion in performing their public duties and rights violations are the exception and not the rule. New legislative restrictions on classroom teaching might undercut the logic of that deferential approach. By adopting such policies, a legislature would be inviting outside scrutiny of how university classes are conducted, and professors may no longer enjoy the same benefit of the doubt when questions are raised about what they said or did in the classroom. Even if judges were to continue to be deferential about the classroom conduct, university administrators are much less likely to do so. Such statutes will impose on the university as an institution an obligation to vouchsafe for the choices its professors make in the classroom, and university officials will need to take steps to do so.

There are some types of classroom conduct that would almost certainly run afoul of policies against compelled belief. Such conduct is probably not common, but undoubtedly there are examples of it to be found – and there are probably many more examples that would be alleged if given legislative encouragement. Interestingly, these types of classroom conduct at best skirt the boundaries of traditional principles of academic freedom, but up to the present there has been little desire to challenge or to defend such practices.

A professor who forced students to participate in specific expressive activities that a student found objectionable would be at risk under such a policy. When high-school students complained to the courts that they were forced to complete community service activities in order to graduate, the court emphasized that the students could choose any activity they liked and were not compelled to contribute their time and energy to a cause or an organization with which they disagreed.[41] Outside the educational context, courts have been quite skeptical of the constitutionality of government mandates requiring that individuals contribute to the expression of ideas with which they disagreed. A professor who rewarded students for participating in particular expressive activities or punished those who did not might well be found to have attempted to compel beliefs. A professor who gave students class credit for attending a protest or rally or assigned them to write letters to government officials in support of a cause specified by the instructor would be at significant risk. Professors could continue to give credit to students for engaging in some civic activity, but the more a professor narrows the range of student choices the more the professor risks being found to have attempted to compel a student to express objectionable political ideas. Professors may generically encourage civic engagement, but they cannot encourage particular issue advocacy.

A professor who required students to make some form of first-person affirmation of a belief or idea would be at risk under such a policy against compelled belief. As we have seen, students can be expected to be able to write or speak from viewpoints with which they disagree. A law student can be required to write persuasive essays from the perspective of Justice Clarence Thomas and of Justice Sonia Sotomayor. So long as such essays or speeches are clearly understood to be exercises in empathetic imagination and strategic advocacy, they cannot be confused with an effort to compel belief. Students can be asked to engage in a faithful pantomime, like a skilled actor or a well-trained lawyer. If, however, a student is

required to make an avowal of his belief in an idea or commitment to a cause, the requirement takes on the characteristics of
the flag salute that the Court found impermissible in *Barnette*.
A professor who required students to "confess their privilege"
or affirm their commitment to inclusivity or acknowledge
their debt to earlier landholders is no longer asking students to
accurately convey their understanding of an idea but is rather
tasking them with making a profession of their belief in an
idea. Such classroom requirements leave no room for critique
or disagreement; they allow only full-throated assent. Students
are not told to examine a proposed idea but to embrace it. As
one court noted, requiring students "to simulate a pledge of
allegiance is serious business," and it is easily read – by both
students and outside observers – as an impermissible effort "to
force orthodoxy."[42]

Similarly, requiring students to make a statement of belief in
some idea crosses the line to compelling belief. Such a required
statement of belief might be either public or private. If public,
the courts have shown particular concern with whether the
person compelled to express the idea would be understood
by others actually to believe in that idea. An actor delivering
a speech on a stage or an orator competing in a contest is
understood by the context to be expressing ideas that he may
or may not share. He is wearing a mask that all can see. An
individual delivering a speech at a rally or holding a sign on the
public square, by contrast, is assumed to be expressing her true
beliefs. For an instructor to force students into such a situation
in which their statements are likely to be understood by others
as sincere expressions runs headlong into the boundaries that
courts have marked out around an individual's right to be free
from compelled speech. Such forced expressions both mark
the speaker as a believer and encourage others to recognize
and accept an apparent orthodoxy. Professors cannot shape
the public discourse by forcing students to conform themselves to the professor's favored views.

Required statements of belief are equally troubling if made privately, though for different reasons. Such private communications do not create the same risk of altering public perceptions, but they do invite the first-order concern that the professor is not satisfied with efforts at persuasion but instead seeks "to coerce uniformity of sentiment." It has occasionally come to public attention that some professors withhold professional opportunities unless students attest to the professor's favored beliefs. Most notably, some science professors are not satisfied that students can perform well on classroom assignments. Before they are willing to write a letter of recommendation or hire a student as a research assistant, they demand that the student affirm their belief in the theory of evolution.[43] In other cases, professors have announced that they will refuse to write letters of recommendation for students with disfavored political views or for activities to which the professor objects.[44] It is an unsettled question whether professors are properly understood to be obliged to write letters of recommendation to all qualified comers. Rather than a duty owed to students, letters of recommendation might be an indulgence to be provided or withheld at will. Conditioning any professional action relative to a student on a demonstration of sincere belief, however, would certainly come under scrutiny under the proposed policies.

Somewhat less certain is the possibility that professors could be subject to investigation on charges of seeking to "indoctrinate" their students rather than teach them. From its very origins, the American Association of University Professors has denied that classroom indoctrination is protected by academic freedom. Little work has been done, however, to unpack that term and identify what would constitute impermissible indoctrination. In practice, universities have been reluctant to scrutinize too carefully what professors do in the classroom and certainly have shown no appetite to discipline professors for the sin of indoctrination. Fear of professors bent on indoctrination has become a staple of conservative critiques of higher education, however. Students who are out of step with the political leanings of the university faculty are prone to think that the faculty is trying to indoctrinate them, even if the faculty would not see it that way.

In laying out a defense of academic freedom in the early days of the University of Chicago, its president William Rainey Harper argued that university professors should be given wide latitude to express their opinion. At the same time, he identified several ways in which a professor could "abuse his privilege of freedom of expression." He contended that "a professor is guilty of an abuse of his privilege who promulgates as truth ideas or opinions that have not been tested scientifically by his colleagues . . . A professor has no right to proclaim to the public as truth discovered that which is yet unsettled and uncertain." Likewise, "a professor abuses his privilege who takes advantage of a classroom exercise to propagate the partisan views of one or another of the political parties. The university is no place for partisanship."[45]

The philosopher John Dewey, a leading force in the creation of the AAUP and the articulation of academic freedom principles in the United States, quoted Harper approvingly and argued that "the university function is the truth-function," and among the highest obligations of the university and of the professors who staff it is "to investigate truth . . . to reach conclusions by means of the best methods at command . . . to communicate this truth to the student." "This is precisely the aim and object of the university." Dewey warned of the great "danger of undue dogmatism and of partisanship" in the universities, and the ever-present temptation "to consecrate ideas born of sheer partisanship with the halo of scientifically established belief." The academic profession should insist "that the individual must be loyal to the truth," but "it is possible to confuse loyalty to truth with self-conceit in the assertion of personal opinion."[46] To do so was both a personal failing in a scholar and an abuse of the privilege of freedom of expression, as Harper would have put it.

The AAUP grappled with the danger of indoctrination in a 2007 report. The report, correctly, insisted that "it is not indoctrination for professors to expect students to comprehend ideas and apply knowledge that is accepted within a relevant discipline." Biology students should be able to understand and explain the theory of evolution. It is not indoctrination for a professor to inform students that in his judgment a controversial theory is the correct one. Professors need the freedom in the classroom to explore, explain, and advance controversial ideas.

> Instructors indoctrinate when they teach particular propositions as *dogmatically* true ... Indoctrination occurs when instructors dogmatically insist on the truth of such propositions by refusing to accord their students the opportunity to contest them. Indoctrination occurs when instructors assert such propositions in ways that prevent students from expressing disagreement. Vigorously to assert a proposition or a viewpoint, however controversial, is to engage in argumentation and discussion – an engagement that lies at the core of academic freedom ... The essence of higher education does not lie in the passive transmission of knowledge but in the inculcation of a mature independence of mind.[47]

Students are entitled to receive the best judgment of their professors, but they are also entitled to be informed when such judgments are controversial, and they should be granted the freedom to engage critically with those judgments.

Indoctrination is not easily visible from the outside. Students are often poorly positioned to judge whether professors are being dogmatic or whether disagreement is adequately tolerated. Reading lists and syllabi provide imperfect clues as to how ideas are addressed in the classroom. The test is not whether professors introduce students to controversial materials and ideas, but whether such materials and ideas are handled in a spirit of open inquiry.

Classroom indoctrination in this sense would likely be prohibited under policies banning the compelling of belief. Students who are reduced to the unquestioning recipients of truths handed down from on high by a professor are being compelled to believe in ways that are analogous to mandatory patriotic exercises. Professors who present students with contested opinions as if they were settled facts misinform them in a manner that seeks to "short-cut" the slow and unsteady path of education and persuasion. A student who complains that a professor is engaged in indoctrination is likely to be ignored on most college campuses. A student who lodges that complaint with such a policy against compelled belief in place would likely necessitate a university investigation into the professor and how she is conducting her classes.

The Problem with Policies against Compelled Belief

If the kind of classroom conduct outlined in this section is already at odds with traditional academic freedom principles, and in some cases at odds with a student's constitutional rights, is there any real danger from legislatures adopting statutes prohibiting such conduct? I think there is.

First, of course, is the need for courts to construe what such a statute actually requires. Courts will be guided by the First Amendment principles articulated by *Barnette* since these proposed policies self-consciously echo those principles, but this is hardly a well-developed area of the law. Courts might interpret such policies as doing very little, since such cases are currently quite rare under existing First Amendment doctrine. Such spare legislative language gives little guidance to future interpreters, and these are not well-settled legal terms of art.

Where there is uncertainty about legal limits, speech is at risk of being chilled.

Second, the penalties associated with these policies risk being very draconian. Texas S.B. 16, for example, simply instructs that "if an institution of higher education determines that a faculty member of the institution has violated this section, the institution shall discharge the faculty member." A single violation of the policy is to be a firing offense. Moreover, many such policies contemplate an end-run around traditional tenure protections. Adjunct and tenured faculty alike might be vulnerable to the unilateral judgment of a university official that they should be immediately dismissed, based on a student complaint and an administrative review. With the possibility of such severe penalties in play, most members of the faculty will attempt to avoid any possibility of facing such a process. Avoiding the risk of student complaints and university investigations would become a very high priority as professors design and conduct their courses. Playing it safe by removing anything from a class that might create even a hint of controversy, or that a student might find objectionable, would become a dominant strategy. The result might be to encourage some professors to change their ways and behave more professionally when dealing with students, but it will also incentivize many professors to be less intellectually stimulating and challenging to their students. The quality of education will suffer because the cost of taking intellectual risks is too high.

Third, such policies add to the growing administrative supervision of faculty teaching, to the likely detriment of academic freedom. S.B. 16 would require that institutions set up an administrative apparatus to collect and investigate complaints of possible violations of the policy. Such policies invite the creation of an intrusive administrative bureaucracy with the power to oversee and punish faculty for what occurs in their classrooms. There is little reason to believe that such an administrative structure will share the professional concerns and norms of the faculty themselves, and thus the scope of academic freedom in the classroom risks being whittled away by university administrators keen to respond to student sensitivities and to political pressure.

Fourth, even these proposals might not survive constitutional scrutiny. These proposals, and enacted policies, do not simply provide a new enforcement mechanism for a preexisting right of students to be free from compelled beliefs. Rather they single out a particular set of beliefs as disfavored. They do not touch the possibility of professors compelling other beliefs, including beliefs that powerful politicians in fact favor. Disfavored ideas get the coercive apparatus of the law, while favored ideas are left unmolested. Professors who attempt to compel their students to believe "critical race theory" are put under the microscope, while professors who attempt to compel their students to believe the theory of evolution are left unaffected by the new laws.

The Supreme Court has been confronted before with laws that single out a subset of impermissible speech for special attention and found them constitutionally wanting. The city of St. Paul, Minnesota, adopted an ordinance criminalizing individuals placing on public or private property a symbol such as a burning cross or Nazi swastika that would arouse alarm on the basis of race, among other characteristics. The Court was unanimous in holding that the ordinance violated the First Amendment, though the justices disagreed as to the reason why. Justice Antonin Scalia's opinion for the Court argued that speech that falls outside the scope of constitutional protection had to be treated in a uniform way. In particular, such "categories of speech [are not] entirely invisible to the Constitution, so that they may be made the vehicles for content discrimination unrelated to their distinctively proscribable content." That is to say, "the government may proscribe libel; but it may not make the further content discrimination of proscribing only libel critical of the government."[48] Not all of the justices agreed with that reasoning at the time, but these policies run into the same potential problem as St. Paul's cross-burning ordinance. Speech that compels belief is outside the scope of constitutional protection (because it violates the constitutional rights of those being compelled), but that does not necessarily mean that the government can single out only some of that speech for punishment. The government could not punish professors who compel their students to believe in the superiority of the Democratic Party but leave untouched professors who compel their students to believe the same about the Republican Party and, arguably, the government is trying to do something similar with these divisive concepts policies.

The constitutional problem with government officials compelling belief is not with the substance of the beliefs in question but with the attempt to compel belief at all. The anti-critical race theory policies are less concerned with protecting students from indoctrination than they are with protecting students from indoctrination into the wrong beliefs. The laws aim at the wrong target and, as a consequence, they have the effect of suppressing ideas, rather than suppressing impermissible conduct. Professors can most safely avoid being investigated and punished under such policies by scrubbing politically disfavored ideas from the curriculum. As a result, such laws cast a pall of orthodoxy over the classroom.

The constitutional challenges of the compelled belief components of the divisive concepts policies are more subtle and potentially less severe than the constitutional infirmities of other components of these policies, but they are nonetheless real. Enforcing these policies would require significant new intrusions into the university classroom and would risk chilling a significant amount of faculty classroom speech that should be permissible under traditional academic freedom and First Amendment principles. The policies invite a great deal of legal uncertainty as to their scope and meaning, and they raise difficult problems of unequal enforcement.

Conclusion

At their best, universities are places in which difficult and controversial ideas can be seriously discussed. Students can encounter and be guided through vast fields of human knowledge and explore the contested claims at the very frontier. Scholars can identify errors in conventional wisdom, shore up and elaborate on our understanding of fundamental features of our natural and social world, and develop new ideas that can reshape our understanding of the world around us. Universities conserve our rich cultural inheritance, but they are also deeply disruptive. Universities shelter critics, skeptics, and radicals, and their insights and arguments will not always be pleasing to the powers that be. Their ideas will not always be correct, but universities should be places where ideas can be freely exchanged and subjected to piercing scrutiny. The currency of the realm should be arguments, and evidence, and analysis, and no idea or belief should be sheltered from criticism and challenge.

Society can often find such hothouses of intellectual freedom to be discomforting, and even threatening but, in the long run, it benefits from nurturing such truth-seeking institutions. A civilization is built on weak foundations if it is unwilling to allow and to respond to criticism. We are better off in knowing and facing the truth rather than blinding ourselves with the illusory security of pleasing falsehoods. Those who are comfortable in the status quo may well find such intellectual ferment to be disorienting, and there is an ever-present temptation to suppress unpleasant and inconvenient truths and to dismiss those who bear the bad news that we have made mistakes, that we are wrong. Preserving intact institutions that are constantly generating nettlesome questions and that are willing to unsettle conventions is no easy task. Institutions of free inquiry are fragile, and they are vulnerable to being tossed and shattered in the storms of passion.

Unfortunately, universities are not always at their best. Universities are often reluctant to act on cases of professional neglect and misconduct in the classroom. The appropriate boundaries of academic freedom that are dictated by the need for germaneness and competence are not always well understood or assiduously observed. The need to respect the intellectual independence of students and to critically engage them rather than coerce them is not always fully appreciated. It is an all-too-human failing to let one's passions and commitments overwhelm one's judgment, and professors are not immune from such lapses.

Fortunately, such professional failures in the classroom are probably much less common than many students or politicians believe. Egregious anecdotes can inflate the sense of the problem. The routine work of teaching that takes place every day in thousands of classrooms across the country does not demand the same public attention as the instances of something going awry. Students are often apt to perceive disagreement or criticism as inspired by political or ideological animus rather than by professional judgment and scholarly skepticism. Even so, universities have a responsibility to address such problems when they occur, and tolerating abuses of academic freedom will tend to degrade the esteem with which it is held and encourage misguided, if well-intentioned, interventions to try to do that which universities will not do themselves.

Academia as a whole has also been neglectful of the need to self-regulate if it is to enjoy the kind of societal respect and deference that the American Association of University Professors called for more than a century ago. Academia can be self-indulgent in the pursuits that it encourages and can be inattentive to the bodies of knowledge that society most needs. The social bargain that professors sought to make with the broader society was that they would be granted some measure of security and independence in exchange for nurturing the kind of expertise and knowledge accumulation that would pay dividends to society at large. The public and their elected representatives are under no obligation to build and maintain expensive institutions of higher education for the benefit of the faculty who work there. For better or for worse, the public will set priorities on types of expertise and knowledge it most values. The professoriate cannot compel the public to value whatever the professoriate itself values. Professors can only seek to persuade their fellow citizens that their pursuits are a worthy investment. Professors have a duty to deliver unpleasant truths, and a society that values knowledge over opinion should seek to nurture truth-seeking and to tolerate discomforting truths. Principles of academic freedom attempt to protect the necessary independence of critical inquiry at the individual level. It shelters the gadfly from recriminations. It allows room for dissidents and iconoclasts. At the institutional level, academia must earn its keep.

Societal trust in academic expertise and the good faith of scholars likewise has to be earned and maintained and cannot simply be assumed. On politically sensitive topics, it is evident that the necessary societal trust in academia is unraveling. No doubt it is particularly difficult to win such trust on such fraught issues. The value of expertise comes from being able to tell people what they need to hear and not necessarily what they want to hear, and it is tempting to shoot the messenger when we do not like the message. Matters are made exponentially more difficult, however, when the professoriate is perceived to be set a world apart from the society that it hopes to serve. Academia tilts sharply to the left, and that has rapidly become much more true in recent decades. If universities are believed to have been captured by a particular political or ideological faction, they will lose their ability to provide trusted neutral expertise and will instead be perceived as and treated as partisans in the political fray. Appeals to academic freedom will likely fall on deaf ears. If academics are believed to have cast their own pall of orthodoxy over state university classrooms, political reform efforts will seem inescapable. Neither society nor universities will be well served if that dynamic takes hold.

Scholarly institutions are fragile. They can be corrupted from within and from without, and the quality of the scholarly product can be debased when free inquiry is curtailed. The First Amendment was not designed to protect universities, but it was designed to protect freedom of thought from demands for social and political conformity. The freedom to dissent is central to the American constitutional experiment and is critical to the functioning of serious institutions of scholarly research and of higher education. Ideas should be debated and discussed and embraced or rejected on the basis of their merits and their persuasive strength. American universities should never seek to shelter favored ideas from careful scrutiny nor suppress disfavored ideas out of fear of how they might be received.

Policies designed to prevent professors from mooting ideas that politicians find disturbing are a repudiation of ideals upon which modern American universities were founded. They run headlong into the constitutional values that the Court acknowledged in the wake of the crusade to ferret out political subversives. They will in time cripple the ability of universities to serve their primary purpose of advancing and disseminating knowledge.

There will always be some ideas that powerholders deem to be subversive. The details of the perceived threat change, but we should hold steadfast to our guiding principles, "that no official, high or petty, can prescribe what shall be orthodox in politics, nationalism, religion, or other matters of opinion."[1]

Further Reading

On the History and Importance of American Universities

Cole, Jonathan R., *The Great American University: Its Rise to Preeminence, Its Indispensable National Role, Why It Must be Protected* (Philadelphia: PublicAffairs, 2012)

Dorn, Charles, *For the Common Good: A New History of Higher Education in America* (Ithaca: Cornell University Press, 2017)

Reuben, Julie A., *The Making of the Modern University* (Chicago: University of Chicago Press, 1996)

Thelin, John R., *A History of American Higher Education* (Baltimore: Johns Hopkins University Press, 2004)

On Academic Freedom in the United States

DelFattore, Joan, *Knowledge in the Making* (New Haven: Yale University Press, 2010)

Downs, Donald Alexander, *Restoring Free Speech and Liberty on Campus* (New York: Cambridge University Press, 2005)

Finkin, Matthew W. and Robert C. Post, *For the Common Good* (New Haven: Yale University Press, 2000)

Fish, Stanley, *Versions of Academic Freedom* (Chicago: University of Chicago Press, 2014)

Heins, Marjorie, *Priests of Our Democracy: The Supreme Court, Academic Freedom, and the Anti-Communist Purge* (New York: New York University Press, 2013)

Post, Robert C., *Democracy, Expertise, and Academic Freedom* (New Haven: Yale University Press, 2012)

Reichman, Henry, *Understanding Academic Freedom* (Baltimore: Johns Hopkins University Press, 2021)

Schrecker, Ellen W., *No Ivory Tower: McCarthyism & the Universities* (New York: Oxford University Press, 1986)

On the First Amendment and the Public University Context

Brettschneider, Corey, *When the State Speaks, What Should It Say? How Democracies Can Protect Expression and Promote Equality* (Princeton: Princeton University Press, 2012)

Chemerinsky, Erwin and Howard Gillman, *Free Speech on Campus* (New Haven: Yale University Press, 2017)

Delgado, Richard and Jean Stefancic, *Must We Defend Nazis? Why the First Amendment Should Not Protect Hate Speech and White Supremacy* (New York: New York University Press, 2018)

Gould, Jon B., *Speak No Evil* (Chicago: University of Chicago Press, 2005)

Norton, Helen, *The Government's Speech and the Constitution* (New York: Cambridge University Press, 2019)

Shiell, Timothy C., *Campus Hate Speech on Trial*, revd. edn. (Lawrence: University Press of Kansas, 2009)

Smolla, Rodney A., *The Constitution Goes to College: Five Constitutional Ideas that Shaped the American University* (New York: New York University Press, 2011)

Strossen, Nadine, *Hate: Why We Should Resist It with Free Speech, Not Censorship* (New York: Oxford University Press, 2018)

Notes

1 The Culture War and the Universities

1 Stop WOKE Act, Action News Jax (December 15, 2021), at 24:15 (https://www.facebook.com/ActionNewsJacksonville/videos/stop-woke-act/663148078398103/).

2 Ibid.; Rachel Fradette, "Gov. Ron DeSantis Signs Education Bills on 'Viewpoint Diversity,' New Civics Curriculum in Florida," *Naples Daily News* (June 22, 2021) (https://www.naplesnews.com/videos/news/local/2021/03/17/desantis-speaks-naples-florida-initiative-expand-civics-education/4734075001/).

3 Mike Pence, "Remarks at the Palmetto Family Council Dinner," C-Span (April 29, 2021) (https://www.c-span.org/video/?510548-1/mike-pence-remarks-palmetto-family-council-dinner); Mike Pence, "Critical Race Theory is State-Sanctioned Racism," *The Hill* (July 17, 2021) (https://www.youtube.com/watch?v=KsB5DPIUASg).

4 Olivia B. Waxman, "'Critical Race Theory is Simply the Latest Bogeyman.' Inside the Fight over What Kids Learn about American History," *Time* (July 16, 2021); "Citizen Pledge," 1776 Action (https://1776action.org/citizen/).

5 "Committee of Counsel on Academic Freedom and Responsibility Resolution Defending Academic Freedom to Teach about Race

and Gender Justice and Critical Race Theory," (February 9, 2022) (https://utexas.app.box.com/s/0dfwoiadkwkww6mksxe4raxzvb 23gzw6); Megan Menchaca, "Lt. Gov. Dan Patrick Pledges to End Tenure for New Hires at Texas Public Universities," *Austin American-Statesman* (February 18, 2022).

6 Jessica Blake, "American Confidence in Higher Ed Hits Historic Low," *Inside Higher Ed* (July 11, 2023).

7 "The Growing Partisan Divide in Views of Higher Education," Pew Research (August 19, 2019) (https://www.pewresearch.org /social-trends/2019/08/19/the-growing-partisan-divide-in- views-of-higher-education-2/).

8 Exec. Order 13950, 3 CFR 433 (2020).

9 Christopher F. Rufo, "'White Fragility' Comes to Washington," *City Journal* (July 18, 2020).

10 https://twitter.com/realchrisrufo/status/1371541044592996352 ?lang=en (March 15, 2021).

11 James Lindsay, *Race Marxism* (Orlando, FL: New Discourses, 2022).

12 AZ Rev Stat § 41–1494 (2022).

13 GA Code § 20–1–11 (2022).

14 N.D. Cent. Code § 15.1–21–05.1 (2023).

15 H.B. 4100 (https://www.scstatehouse.gov/sess124_2021–2022 /appropriations2021/tap1b.pdf).

16 Tex. Educ. Code § 21.4555 (2023).

17 John Kennedy, "DeSantis' 'Stop WOKE Act' Faces Court Test as Universities Become Targets. At Issue: Free Speech," *Florida Times-Union* (June 19, 2022).

18 H.B. 7 (https://www.flsenate.gov/Session/Bill/2022/7/BillText /er/PDF); Fla. Stat. § 1000.05(4) (2023).

19 The Stop WOKE Act was enjoined by a federal district court. Pernell v. Florida Board of Governors of the State University System, 641 F.Supp. 3d 1218 (Dist. N. FL 2022).

20 James Copland, "How to Regulate Critical Race Theory in Schools: A Primer and Model Legislation," Manhattan Institute Issue Brief (August 2021), 7; Christopher F. Rufo, Ilya Shapiro,

and Matt Beienburg, "Abolish DEI Bureaucracies and Restore Colorblind Equality in Public Universities," Manhattan Institute Issue Brief (January 2023).

21 "CRT Forward: Tracking the Attack on Critical Race Theory," Critical Race Studies Program, UCLA School of Law (April 6, 2023) (https://crtforward.law.ucla.edu/wp-content/uploads/2023/04/UCLA-Law_CRT-Report_Final.pdf); "America's Censored Classrooms 2023," PEN America (November 9, 2023) (https://pen.org/report/americas-censored-classrooms-2023/).

22 Idaho Code § 33–138 (2023).

23 Kate McGee, "Lt. Gov. Dan Patrick Proposes Ending University Tenure to Combat Critical Race Theory Teachings," *Texas Tribune* (February 18, 2022).

24 Valeria Olivares and Talia Richman, "Dan Patrick Wants to Fight Critical Race Theory by Ending Tenure at Texas' Colleges, Universities," *Dallas Morning News* (February 18, 2022).

25 Christopher F. Rufo, "The Great University Reform Debate," (May 21, 2023) (https://christopherrufo.com/p/the-great-university-reform-debate).

2 Academic Freedom in the United States

1 "The Origin of Races," *Nashville Daily American* (January 6, 1878): 2.

2 Alexander Winchell, "Science Gagged in Nashville," *Nashville Daily American* (June 16, 1878): 2.

3 Ibid.

4 "'Heresy' at Vanderbilt," *Nashville Daily American* (June 16, 1878): 2.

5 "Prof. Winchell's Heresy," *Nashville Daily American* (July 12, 1878): 4.

6 "A Defense of the Vanderbilt," *Atlanta Daily Constitution* (August 23, 1878): 2. On the Winchell affair, see also Mary Engel, "A Chapter in the History of Academic Freedom: The Case of Alexander Winchell," *History of Education Journal* 10 (1959): 73.

7 "Yale as a Battle-Ground," *New York Times* (April 4, 1880), 1.

8 Harris E. Starr, *William Graham Sumner* (New York: Henry Holt and Company, 1925), 359, 365, 362. See also, John D. Heyl and Barbara S. Heyl, "The Sumner-Porter Controversy at Yale: Pre-Paradigmatic Sociology and Institutional Crisis," *Sociological Inquiry* 46 (1976): 41; Walter P. Metzger, *Academic Freedom in the Age of the University* (New York: Columbia University Press, 1955), 61–64.

9 James Woodrow, "Inaugural Address," *Southern Presbyterian Review* 14 (January 1862): 510, 519.

10 Clement Eaton, "Professor James Woodrow and the Freedom of Teaching in the South," *Journal of Southern History* 28 (1962): 13.

11 William E. Ellis, "Frank LeRond McVey His Defense of Academic Freedom," *Register of the Kentucky Historical Society* 67 (1969): 43.

12 Frank L. McVey, *The Gates Open Slowly* (Lexington: University Press of Kentucky, 1949), 292, 294.

13 James R. Montgomery and Gerald Gaither, "Evolution and Education in Tennessee: Decisions and Dilemmas," *Tennessee Historical Quarterly* 28 (1969): 144. See also, Kimberly Ann Marinucci, "Probing the Nation: Americanism, Public Universities, and the Politics of Academic Freedom, 1918–1946" (Ph.D. dissertation, SUNY Stony Brook, 2001).

14 Marinucci, 53, 54.

15 *Tennessee Public Acts* (1925), Chapter No. 27, H.B. 185, 50–51.

16 Thomas Elmer Will, "The Value of Academic Opinions on Economic Questions," *The Industrialist* 24 (1898): 602.

17 "Comment by E.A. Ross, University of Wisconsin," *Papers and Proceedings of the American Sociological Society* 9 (1915): 166. On the chilling effect, see Wieman v. Updegraff, 344 U.S. 183, 195 (1952); New York Times v. Sullivan, 376 U.S. 254, 300 (1964). On self-censorship, see James L. Gibson and Joseph L. Sutherland, "Keeping Your Mouth Shut: Spiraling Self-Censorship in the United States," *Political Science Quarterly* (2023); Greg Lukianoff

and Rikki Schlott, *The Canceling of the American Mind* (New York: Simon & Schuster, 2023).

18　Upton Sinclair, *The Goose-Step* (Pasadena, CA: Upton Sinclair, 1923), 399.

19　On the Ross affair, see James C. Mohr, "Academic Turmoil and Public Opinion: The Ross Case at Stanford," *Pacific Historical Review* 39 (1970): 39; Laurence R. Veysey, *The Emergence of the American University* (Chicago: University of Chicago Press, 1965), 400–407; Walter P. Metzger, *Academic Freedom in the Age of the University* (New York: Columbia University Press, 1955), 162–172.

20　Henry Philip Tappan, *University Education* (New York: George P. Putnam, 1850), 99, 42.

21　The Carnegie Foundation for the Advancement of Teaching, *Third Annual Report of the President and Treasurer* (New York: D.B. Updike, 1908), 89, 82, 86, 87.

22　American Association of University Professors, "1915 Declaration of Principles on Academic Freedom and Tenure," in *Policy Documents and Reports*, 11th edn. (Baltimore: Johns Hopkins University Press, 2015), 5, 6.

23　For the early history of the AAUP and its investigations, see Matthew W. Finkin and Robert C. Post, *For the Common Good* (New Haven: Yale University Press, 2009); Walter P. Metzger, *Academic Freedom in the Age of the University* (New York: Columbia University Press, 1955); Hans-Joerg Tiede, *University Reform* (Baltimore: Johns Hopkins University Press, 2015); David M. Rabban, *The Meaning of Academic Freedom* (Cambridge: Harvard University Press, 2024).

24　"1940 Statement of Principles on Academic Freedom and Tenure," in AAUP, *Policy Documents and Reports*, 13.

3　The Era of the Loyalty Oaths

1　Charles J. Holden, *The New Southern University* (Lexington: University Press of Kentucky, 2012), 52, 55, 60.

2　Holden, 134, 135.

3 Robert F. Durden, "Crises in University Governance: The Launching of Duke University, 1925–1935: Part II: 1930–1935," *North Carolina Historical Review* 64 (1987): 418–419.

4 David Clark, "Communism and Socialism at Chapel Hill," (August 12, 1940) (https://exhibits.lib.unc.edu/items/show/163).

5 On the First Red Scare, see Robert K. Murray, *Red Scare* (Minneapolis: University of Minnesota Press, 1955); Todd Pfannestiel, *Rethinking the Red Scare* (New York: Routledge, 2003); Jacob Kramer, *The New Freedom and the Radicals* (Philadelphia: Temple University Press, 2015).

6 *New York Laws* (1902), chap. 370.

7 *West Virginia Acts* (1919), chap. 24.

8 Thorstein Veblen, "In Charge of the Reconstruction Program," *The Dial* 65 (November 30, 1918): 497.

9 Joint Legislative Committee Investigating Seditious Activities, *Revolutionary Radicalism*, vol. 1 (Albany, NY: J.B. Lyon Company, 1920), 14, 15, 16, 17.

10 Lawrence H. Chamberlain, *Loyalty and Legislative Action* (Ithaca: Cornell University Press, 1951), 40.

11 Alfred E. Smith, *Public Papers of Alfred E. Smith, Governor* (Albany, NY: J.B. Lyon Co., 1921), 369, 370.

12 *New York Laws* (1921), chap. 666.

13 *Pennsylvania Laws* (1921), No. 351.

14 American Civil Liberties Union, *The Gag on Teaching* (New York City: American Civil Liberties Union, 1931), 4, 17.

15 *New York Laws* (1939), chap. 547, as amended *New York Laws* (1940), chap. 564.

16 Taylor v. State, 194 Miss. 1, 44, 33, 38 (Miss. 1943).

17 Harold M. Hyman, *To Try Men's Souls* (Berkeley: University of California Press, 1959), 338.

18 Thurman Arnold, "How *Not* to Get Investigated," *Harper's Magazine* (November 1948): 61, 62.

19 *New York Laws* (1949), chap. 360.

20 Matter of L'Hommedieu v. Board of Regents, 276 App. Div. 494, 505 (N.Y. 3rd Dept. 1950).

21 ACLU, *The Gag on Teaching*, 23, 24.

22 In the Matter of Kay v. Board of Education, New York City, 173 Misc. 943, 947, 948 (N.Y. Misc. 1940).

23 Quoted in Jane Sanders, *Cold War on the Campus* (Seattle: University of Washington Press, 1979), 16.

24 Ibid., 20.

25 Letter to Robert Gordon Sproul, July 18, 1950 (https://oac.cdlib .org/view?docId=hb0d5nb3d2&brand=oac4).

26 On the California loyalty oath, see David P. Gardner, *The California Oath Controversy* (Berkeley: University of California Press, 1967); George R. Stewart, *The Year of the Oath* (Garden City, NY: Doubleday, 1950).

27 *Texas Laws* (1953), chap. 41.

28 *Investigation of Communist Activities in the Los Angeles Area – Part 1: Hearings before the Committee on Un-American Activities*, 83rd Cong., 1st sess. (1953), 520.

29 Daniman v. Board of Education, 306 N.Y. 532, 538 (N.Y. 1954).

30 On universities during the Second Red Scare, see Ellen W. Schrecker, *No Ivory Tower* (New York: Oxford University Press, 1986); M.J. Heale, *McCarthy's Americans* (London: Macmillan, 1998); William J. Billingsley, *Communists on Campus* (Chapel Hill: University of North Carolina Press, 2017); Jeff Woods, *Black Struggle, Red Scare* (Baton Rouge: Louisiana State University, 2004).

31 William Conklin, "Eisenhower Says Farewell to Columbia University," *New York Times* (January 17, 1953), 1, 6.

32 Quoted in Schrecker, 111.

33 Association of American Universities, "The Rights and Responsibilities of Universities and their Faculties," *University Bulletin* [California] 1 (April 20, 1953): 161, 162.

34 Quoted in Schrecker, 110.

35 Raymond B. Allen, "Communists Should Not Teach in American Colleges," *Educational Forum* 13 (1949): 433, 444.

36 Sidney Hook, *Political Power and Personal Freedom* (New York: Criterion Books, 1959), 298, 306.

37 Arthur O. Lovejoy, "Communism *versus* Academic Freedom," *The American Scholar* 18 (1949): 332.

38 Adler v. Board of Education of the City of New York, 342 U.S. 485, 493 (1952).

4 The First Amendment Comes to Campus

1 "A Radical Professor," *Washington Post* (June 23, 1915): 6; "Furor is Created at Penn City," *Cincinnati Enquirer* (June 20, 1915): 13; "Penn Graduates Here Have Little Pity for Nearing," *New York Tribune* (June 23, 1915), 5.

2 "Is the College Professor a 'Hired Man'?" *Literary Digest* (July 10, 1915): 65; Lichtner Witmer, *The Nearing Case* (New York: B.W. Huebsch, 1915), 17; Charles Willis Thompson, "The Truth about Nearing's Case," *New York Times* (July 18, 1915): SM4.

3 "Is the College Professor a 'Hired Man'?'; Witmer, 69; "Dr. Nearing Out for Good; Unfit, Insist Trustees," *New York Tribune* (October 12, 1915): 4.

4 M.M. Chambers, "Legal Aspects of Personnel Administration in State Colleges," *Personnel Journal* 11 (1932): 100.

5 Alexander Brody, *The American State and Higher Education* (Washington, D.C.: American Council on Education, 1935), 144, 134.

6 Gillan v. Board of Regents, 88 Wis. 7, 14, 10 (Wis. 1894).

7 Lindley v. Davis, 117 Kan. 58, 560 (Kan. 1925).

8 Theodore C. Sorensen, "Legislative Control of Loyalty in the School System," *Nebraska Law Review* 29 (1950): 491.

9 West Virginia Board of Education v. Barnette, 319 U.S. 624, 642 (1943).

10 Thompson v. Wallin, 196 Misc. 686, 701, 706 (N.Y. Sup. Ct. 1949).

11 "Judicial Review and the Feinberg Law – The Presumption of Validity," *Illinois Law Review* 45 (1950): 279.

12 United Public Workers v. Mitchell, 330 U.S. 75, 101, 102 (1947).

13 Thorp v. Board of Trustees, 6 N.J. 498, 512 (NJ 1951).

14 Board of Regents v. Updegraff, 205 Okla. 301, 305–306 (Okla. 1951).

15 Thompson v. Wallin, 301 NY 476, 489, 492 (NY 1950).

16 People v. Crane, 214 NY 154, 168 (NY 1915).

17 "Speeches at Commencement Luncheon," *Columbia Alumni News* 8 (July 1917): 883.

18 "Loyalty in the Classroom," *The Editorial* 2 (April 14, 1917): 690.

19 Carol S. Gruber, *Mars and Minerva* (Baton Rouge: Louisiana State University, 1975), 256. See also, Timothy Reese Cain, *Establishing Academic Freedom* (New York: Palgrave Macmillan, 2012); John K. Wilson, *Patriotic Correctness* (New York: Routledge, 2008).

20 See also William W. Van Alstyne, "Academic Freedom and the First Amendment in the Supreme Court of the United States: An Unhurried Historical Review," *Law & Contemporary Problems* 53 (1990): 79.

21 Abrams v. United States, 250 U.S. 616, 630 (1919) (Holmes, J., dissenting).

22 Gitlow v. New York, 268 U.S. 652, 673 (1925) (Holmes, J., dissenting).

23 United States v. Schwimmer, 279 U.S. 644, 655, 654 (1929) (Holmes, J., dissenting).

24 Whitney v. California, 274 U.S. 357, 375 (1927) (Brandeis, J., concurring).

25 Stromberg v. California, 283 U.S. 359, 369 (1931).

26 *Holmes-Laski Letters*, ed. Mark De Wolfe Howe, vol. 2 (Cambridge: Harvard University Press, 1953), 1250.

27 Ibid., vol. 2, 1250; Ibid., vol. 1, 115–116.

28 On Holmes's intellectual circle, see Brad Snyder, *The House of Truth* (New York: Oxford University Press, 2017); Louis Menand, *The Metaphysical Club* (New York: Farrar, Straus and Giroux, 2001); David M. Rabban, *Free Speech in Its Forgotten Years* (New York: Cambridge University Press, 1997); G. Edward White, *Justice Oliver Wendell Holmes* (New York: Oxford University Press, 1993); Mark A. Graber, *Transforming Free Speech* (Berkeley: University of California Press, 1991).

29 Martin v. City of Struthers, 319 U.S. 141, 150 (1943) (Murphy, J., concurring).

30 West Virginia State Board of Education v. Barnette, 319 U.S. 624, 642 (1942).

31 McAuliffe v. Mayor and Board of Aldermen of New Bedford, 155 Mass. 216, 220 (1892).

32 Adler v. Board of Education of City of New York, 342 U.S. 485, 492 (1952).

33 Adler v. Board of Education of City of New York, 342 U.S. 485, 508 (1952) (Douglas, J., dissenting).

34 Ibid., 509, 510.

35 Adler v. Board of Education of City of New York, 342 U.S. 485, 497 (1952) (Black, J., dissenting).

36 William O. Douglas, "The Bill of Rights is Not Enough," *New York University Law Review* 38 (1963): 213, 212.

37 Hugo L. Black, "The Bill of Rights," *New York University Law Review* 35 (1960): 880–881.

38 Wieman v. Updegraff, 344 U.S. 183, 191 (1952).

39 Frankfurter had dissented in *Adler*, but there he had thought the case was not yet ripe for a constitutional argument and so did not join the opinions of Douglas and Black.

40 Wieman v. Updegraff. 195, 196, 197.

41 *Tax Exempt Foundations: Hearings Before the Select Committee to Investigate Tax-Exempt Foundations and Comparable Organizations*, 82nd Cong., 2nd sess., 291, 292, 293 (1952).

42 Sweezy v. New Hampshire, 354 U.S. 234, 250, 251 (1957). This was not an uncommon strategy for the Warren Court. See Keith E. Whittington, *Repugnant Laws* (Lawrence: University Press of Kansas, 2019), 22.

43 Sweezy v. New Hampshire, 354 U.S. 234, 261, 262, 263 (1957) (Frankfurter, J., concurring). Frankfurter was quoting from Conference of Representatives of the University of Cape Town and the University of Witwatersrand, *The Open Universities in South Africa* (Cape Town: 1957). The statement was the product of a conference organized to protest the imposition of racial apartheid on the theretofore color-blind universities.

44 Joy Ann-Williamson-Lott, *Jim Crow Campus* (New York:

Teachers College Press, 2018), 60–68; Woods, *Black Struggle, Red Scare*, 70–77.

45 Shelton v. Tucker, 364 U.S. 479, 485, 487 (1960).
46 Shelton v. Tucker, 364 U.S. 479, 490, 496 (1960) (Frankfurter, J., dissenting).
47 Frankfurter was understating the impact that Act 10 had already had on university campuses in the state.
48 C. Vann Woodward, "The Unreported Crisis in the Southern Colleges," *Harper's Magazine* (September 30, 1962), 82.
49 Keyishian v. Board of Regents, 385 U.S. 589, 595, 599, 600, 601 (1967).
50 Keyishian v. Board of Regents, 601–602, 603, 604.
51 Epperson v. Arkansas, 393 U.S. 97, 107 (1968).
52 Paul Horwitz, *First Amendment Institutions* (Cambridge: Harvard University Press, 2013). See also, Jonathan Rauch, *The Constitution of Knowledge* (Washington, D.C.: Brookings Institution, 2021).

5 The Professor as a Government Employee

1 Defendants' Response in Opposition to Plaintiffs' Motion for a Preliminary Injunction, Pernell v. Florida Board of Governors, U.S. Dist. Ct. N. Dist. Florida (September 22, 2022), 2.
2 Edwards v. California University of Pennsylvania, 156 F.3d 488, 491 (3rd Cir. 1998).
3 Kirkland v. Northside Independent School District, 890 F.2d 794, 800 (5th Cir. 1989).
4 Pickering v. Board of Education of Township High School District 205, 391 U.S. 563 (1968).
5 Pickering v. Board of Education, 36 Ill. 2d 568, 577 (Ill. 1967).
6 Pickering v. Board of Education of Township High School District 205, 391 U.S. 563, 568 (1968).
7 Ibid., 568, 572, 573.
8 Perry v. Sindermann, 408 U.S. 593 (1972).
9 Connick v. Myers, 461 U.S. 138, 143, 144, 146, 147, 149, 154, 147, 152 (1983).

10 Garcetti v. Ceballos, 547 U.S. 410, 415 (2006).

11 Ibid., 419

12 Ibid., 421, 422, 424.

13 Ibid., 438.

14 Ibid., 425.

15 Rosenberger v. Rector & Visitors of the University of Virginia, 515 U.S. 819, 835 (1995).

16 Garcetti, 425.

17 Keyishian, 603.

18 Adler, 497.

19 Pickering, 573.

20 Keyishian, 603.

21 Wieman, 197.

22 Adler, 501.

23 Sweezy, 261, 250.

24 See also, Keith E. Whittington, *Speak Freely* (Princeton: Princeton University Press, 2018); Keith E. Whittington, "Academic Freedom and the Mission of the University," *Houston Law Review* 59 (2022): 821.

25 Miller v. California, 413 U.S. 15, 24 (1973).

26 Red Lion Broadcasting, Inc. v. FCC, 395 U.S. 367, 390 (1969).

27 "1940 Statement of Principles on Academic Freedom and Tenure," in AAUP, *Policy Documents and Reports*, 13.

28 See also, Keith E. Whittington, "What Can Professors Say on Campus? Intramural Speech and the First Amendment," *Journal of Free Speech Law* (forthcoming).

29 Keddie v. Pennsylvania State University, 412 F.Supp. 1264, 1270 (M.D. Pa. 1976).

30 Traditional *Pickering* balancing as it has been applied by the courts is not sufficiently sensitive to the unique concerns of the academic context. For more detail of how *Pickering* balancing should be performed when professors are speaking outside the scope of their employment duties, see Keith E. Whittington, "What Can Professors Say in Public? Extramural Speech and the First Amendment," *Case Western Reserve Law Review* 73 (2023).

The considerations discussed there are applicable to the context of speech within the scope of their employment duties as well.

31 AAUP, Statement of Principle, 13.

32 Kracunas v. Iona College, 119 F.3d 80, 88 (2nd Circuit 1997).

33 Bonnell v. Lorenzo, 241 F.3d 800, 818 n.10, 820–821 (2nd Circuit 2001).

34 Hardy v. Jefferson Community College, 260 F.3d 671, 679 (6th Circuit 2001).

35 Meriwether v. Hartop, 992 F.3d 492, 506, 507 (6th Circuit 2021). The state university adopted a policy requiring that university officials, including professors, refer to students by their "preferred pronoun[s]" reflecting the students' "self-asserted gender identity."

36 Ibid., 508, 511. It is not obvious that the court's judgment about the application of those principles to the facts of this case is fully justified. The university employer's interest in how professors address students in the classroom is relatively strong.

37 For doubts about constitutionalizing individual academic freedom because of the problem of judges assessing the quality of scholarly work, *see* Lawrence Rosenthal, "Does the First Amendment Protect Academic Freedom?" *Journal of College and University Law* 46 (2021): 223.

38 American Association of University Professors, "1915 Declaration of Principles on Academic Freedom and Tenure," in *Policy Documents and Reports*, 11th edn. (Baltimore: Johns Hopkins University Press, 2015), 9.

39 American Association of University Professors, "Academic Freedom and Tenure in the Quest for National Security," *AAUP Bulletin* 42 (1956): 49, 58.

40 Robert C. Post, *Democracy, Expertise, Academic Freedom* (New Haven: Yale University Press, 2012), 48.

41 Planned Parenthood of the Heartland v. Heineman, 724 F. Supp. 2d 1025, 1048 (D. Neb. 2010).

42 Planned Parenthood Minnesota, North Dakota, South Dakota v. Rounds, 530 F.3d 724, 735 (8th Circuit 2008).

43 National Institute of Family & Life Advocates v. Becerra, 138 S.Ct. 2361, 2374 (2018).

44 Private extramural speech that is professionally incompetent might well raise questions about professional fitness for an academic position. The AAUP emphasizes that extramural speech should not be the sole basis for determining that a professor is professionally unfit but it might well lead a university to, for example, take a closer look at that faculty member's scholarship and classroom speech to insure that it is professionally competent. American Association of University Professors, "Committee A Statement on Extramural Utterances," in *Policy Documents and Reports*, 11th edn. (Baltimore: Johns Hopkins University Press, 2015), 31 ("Extramural utterances rarely bear upon the faculty member's fitness for continuing service. Moreover, a final decision should take into account the faculty member's entire record as a teacher and scholar.").

45 United States v. National Treasury Employees Union, 513 U.S. 454, 467 (1995).

46 Lane v. Franks, 573 U.S. 228, 240 (2014).

47 Pickering, 568, 572.

48 Helget v. City of Hays, 844 F.3d 1216, 1221 (10th Circuit 2017).

49 Martin v. Parrish, 805 F.2d 583, 586 (5th Circuit 1986).

50 Engquist v. Oregon Department of Agriculture, 478 F.3d 985, 994 (9th Circuit 2007).

51 AAUP, 1915 Declaration of Principles, 6.

52 Koch v. Hutchinson, 847 F.2d 1436, 1442 (10th Circuit 1988).

53 Egger v. Phillips, 710 F.2d 292, 317, 318 (7th Circuit 1983).

54 Wren v. Spurlock, 798 .2d 1313, 1319 (10th Circuit 1986).

55 On academic freedom principles and professional incompetence, *see* Brain G. Brooks, "Adequate Cause for Dismissal: The Missing Element in Academic Freedom," *Journal of College and University Law* 22 (1995): 331; David M. Rabban, "The Regrettable Underenforcement of Incompetence as Cause to Dismiss Tenured Faculty," *Indiana Law Journal* 91 (2015): 39.

56 Rankin v. McPherson, 483 U.S. 378, 389 (1987).

57 Hiers v. Board of Regents of the University of North Texas System, Civil No. 4:20–CV-321–SDJ, 25–26 (E.D. Tex. 2022).
58 Davis v. West Community Hospital, 755 F.2d 455, 461 (5th Circuit 1985).

6 Teaching in the Government School

1 Johanns v. Livestock Marketing Association, 544 U.S. 550, 557 (2005).
2 Pleasant Grove City v. Summum, 555 U.S. 460, 467 (2009).
3 National Endowment for the Arts v. Finley, 524 U.S. 569, 598 (1998) (Scalia, J., concurring in judgment).
4 West Virginia Board of Education v. Barnette, 319 U.S. 624, 631 (1943).
5 Cal. Educ. Code § 51204.5; Cal. Educ. Code § 60044.
6 Steven Shiffrin, "Government Speech," 27 *UCLA Law Review* 27 (1980): 565, 568n11.
7 Wooley v. Maynard, 430 U.S. 705, 717 (1977).
8 Shurtleff v. City of Boston, 142 S. Ct. 1583, 1595–1596 (2022) (Alito, J., concurring in the judgment).
9 Pleasant Grove City v. Summum, 555 U.S. 460, 473 (2009).
10 Shurtleff, 1596.
11 Defendants' Response in Opposition to Plaintiffs' Motion for a Preliminary Injunction, Pernell v. Florida Board of Governors, U.S. Dist. Ct. N. Dist. Florida (September 22, 2022), 10.
12 Mayer v. Monroe County Community School Corp., 474 F.3d 477, 479 (7th Cir. 2007).
13 Ibid., 480.
14 Shurtleff, 1595.
15 Shurtleff, 1589.
16 Shurtleff, 1596.
17 Walker v. Texas Division, Sons of Confederate Veterans, 576 U.S. 200, 211, 213 (2015); Summum, 472.
18 California Const. Art. IX, § 9 (1879).
19 James B. Angell, *Selected Addresses* (New York: Longmans, Green, and Co., 1912), 30, 29, 31.

20 Andrew Sloan Draper, *American Education* (Boston: Houghton Mifflin, 1909), 197.

21 *The Cornell University Register, 1869–1870* (Ithaca, NY: Cornell University Press, 1870), 21.

22 *The Jubilee of the University of Wisconsin* (Madison, WI: Jubilee Committee, 1905), 123.

23 Johanns, 560.

24 Summum, 472.

25 Angell, 31.

26 Summum, 472.

27 Page v. Lexington County School District One, 531 F.3d 275, 282 (4th Circuit 2008).

28 Matal v. Tam, 528 U.S. 218, 236 (2017).

29 Walker, 222.

30 Shurtleff, 1598.

31 On Levinson's reluctance to teach *Marbury*, *see* Sanford Levinson, "Why I Do Not Teach Marbury (Except to Eastern Europeans) and Why You Shouldn't Either," *Wake Forest Law Review* 38 (2003): 553.

32 Kennedy v. Bremerton School District, 142 S. Ct. 2407, 2424 (2022).

33 Ibid., 2425.

34 Keyishian, 603.

35 Wieman, 195.

36 Meriwether, 507.

37 On the value of a transparency requirement for government speech, see Helen Norton, *The Government's Speech and the Constitution* (New York: Cambridge University Press, 2019), 43–49.

38 Clark v. Community for Creative Non-Violence, 468 U.S. 288, 293 (1984).

39 Evans-Marshall v. Board of Education of Tipp City Exempted Village School District, 624 F.3d 332, 340 (6th Circuit 2010).

40 For skepticism that even primary and secondary schools should be understood as pure instruments of government speech, see

Mark G. Yudof, *When Government Speaks* (Berkeley: University of California Press, 1983), 215–218.

41 Evans-Marshall v. Board of Education of Tipp City Exempted Village School District, 624 F.3d 332, 341, 342 (6th Cir. 2010).

42 AAUP, 1915 Declaration of Principles, 4.

7 Compelling Students to Believe

1 Executive Order No. 13950, 3. C.F.R. 433 (2021), §7(b), §4(1).

2 Fla. Stat. § 1000.05(4)(a) (2023).

3 S.B. No. 16, §3 (2023).

4 Pernell v. Florida Board of Governors of the State University System, 641 F. Supp. 3d 1218, 1251n27 (Dist. N. Fl. 2022).

5 A prohibition on speech that "inculcates" an idea might be synonymous with speech that either "promotes" or "compels" belief in that idea. If a policy were adopted that prohibited only the inculcation of a disfavored idea, universities and judges would be faced with a difficult task of interpreting such a stand-alone prohibition.

6 Tinker v. Des Moines Independent Community School District, 393 U.S. 503, 506 (1969).

7 On the Jehovah's Witnesses and the flag case, see Shawn Francis Peters, *Judging Jehovah's Witnesses* (Lawrence: University Press of Kansas, 2000); David Manwaring, *Render unto Caesar* (Chicago: University of Chicago Press, 1962); Jerry Bergman, "The Modern Religious Objection to Mandatory Flag Salute in America: A History and Evaluation," *Journal of Church and State* 39 (1997): 215.

8 Minersville School District v. Gobitis, 310 U.S. 586, 594, 600 (1940). The Gobitas family name was misspelled in the court records.

9 Ibid., 603, 601, 604, 606.

10 Peters, 57.

11 Peters, 96.

12 Jones v. Opelika, 316 U.S. 584, 624 (1942) (Black, Douglas, and Murphy, J.J., dissenting).

13　West Virginia State Board of Education v. Barnette, 319 U.S. 624, 646–647 (1943) (Frankfurter, J., dissenting).

14　Zechariah Chafee, *Free Speech in the United States* (Cambridge: Harvard University Press, 1948), 399.

15　Peters, 253.

16　West Virginia State Board of Education, 631.

17　Ibid., 631, 633n13, 633.

18　Ibid., 634, 637, 640, 641, 642.

19　Miami Herald Publishing Co. v. Tornillo, 418 U.S. 241 (1974); Keller v. State Bar of California, 496 U.S. 1 (1990).

20　Wooley v. Maynard, 430 U.S. 705 (1977).

21　Hurley v. Irish-American Gay, Lesbian and Bisexual Group of Boston, 515 U.S. 557 (1995); National Institute of Family and Life Advocates v. Becerra, 138 S.Ct. 2361 (2017).

22　Rumsfeld v. Forum for Academic and Institutional Rights, 547 U.S. 47, 61 (2006).

23　Turner Broadcasting System, Inc. v. Federal Communications Commission, 512 U.S. 622, 641 (1994); CN v. Ridgewood Board of Education, 430 F.3d 159, 186, 187 (3rd Cir. 2005).

24　Brown v. Li, 308 F.3d 939, 953 (9th Cir. 2002).

25　Lipp v. Morris, 579 F.2d 834 (3rd Cir. 1978).

26　Holloman ex rel. Holloman v. Harland, 370 F.3d 1252 (11th Cir. 2004).

27　Brinsdon v. McAllen Independent School District, 863 F.3d 338 (5th Cir. 2017); Oliver v. Arnold, 3 F.4th 152 (5th Cir. 2021).

28　Fleming v. Jefferson County School District R-1, 298 F.3d 918, 925 (10th Cir. 2002).

29　Hazelwood School District v. Kuhlmeier, 484 U.S. 260, 273 (1988).

30　Settle v. Dickson County School Board, 53 F.3d 152, 155, 156 (6th Cir. 1995).

31　Ward v. Polite, 667 F.3d 727, 733 (6th Cir. 2012).

32　Axson-Flynn v. Johnson, 356 F.3d 1277, 1292, 1293 (10th Cir. 2004).

33　Hazelwood, 278.

34 Ambach v. Norwick, 441 U.S. 68, 77 (1979).

35 Mayer, 480.

36 West Virginia Board of Education, 631, 632n12, 633, 634, 637, 640.

37 Steirer v. Bethlehem Area School District, 987 F.2d 989, 994, 996, 997 (3rd Cir. 1993).

38 Oliver, 163, 166.

39 Brinsdon v. McAllen Independent School District, 863 F.3d 338, 349, 350 (5th Cir. 2017).

40 Axson-Flynn, 1282.

41 Steirer, 996.

42 Brinsdon, 350.

43 Nick Madigan, "Professor's Snub of Creationists Prompts U.S. Inquiry," *New York Times* (February 3, 2003): A11.

44 Scott Jaschik, "Politics, Education and Letters of Recommendation," *Inside Higher Ed* (April 24, 2019).

45 William Rainey Harper, "Freedom of Speech," *University Record* 5 (January 18, 1901), 377.

46 John Dewey, "Academic Freedom," *The Middle Works, 1899–1924*, vol. 2, ed. Jo Ann Boydston (Carbondale: Southern Illinois University Press, 1976), 55, 58, 59, 60.

47 AAUP, "Freedom in the Classroom," in *Policy Documents and Reports*, 11th edn. (Baltimore: Johns Hopkins University Press, 2015), 20, 21.

48 R.A.V. v. St. Paul, 505 U.S. 377, 384 (1992).

Conclusion

1 West Virginia Board of Education v. Barnette, 319 U.S. 624, 642 (1943).

Index